Reading Visual Poetry

Reading Visual Poetry

Willard Bohn

Madison • Teaneck
Fairleigh Dickinson University Press

Published by Fairleigh Dickinson University Press
Co-published with The Rowman & Littlefield Publishing Group, Inc.
4501 Forbes Boulevard, Suite 200, Lanham, Maryland 20706
www.rlpgbooks.com

Estover Road, Plymouth PL6 7PY, United Kingdom

First paperback edition 2013

British Library Cataloguing in Publication Information Available

Library of Congress Cataloging-in-Publication Data

The hardback edition of this book was previously cataloged by the Library of Congress as follows:

Bohn, Willard, 1939–
Reading visual poetry / Willard Bohn.
p. cm.
Includes bibliographical references and index.
1. Visual poetry—History and criticism. 2. Poetry—Explication. I. Title.
PN1455.B64 2010
809.1'04—dc22
2010008445

ISBN: 978-1-61147-062-8 (cloth)
ISBN: 978-1-61147-615-6 (pbk.)
ISBN: 978-1-61147-063-5 (electronic)

™

Contents

Illustrations

Acknowledgments

MOST OF CHAPTER 4 WAS WRITTEN IN ENGLAND DURING THE FIRST three months of 2008. I would like to thank the Institute of Advanced Study, Durham University, for awarding me a distinguished research fellowship. I am grateful as well to the Wolfsonian Museum, Florida International University, for a visiting research fellowship in 2005 that enabled me to conduct preliminary research for chapter 5. Thanks also to Eduardo Kac for permission to reproduce three images in chapter 7. Earlier versions of several sections appeared in the following publications and are reprinted with their kind permission: "Three Spanish Ultraist Poets," *Revue des Littératures del l'Union Européen,* no. 8 (December 2008), 13–27; "Visual Poetry in France after Apollinaire," *Insights* 1, no. 9 (2008), 2–13; "Exploring the Concrete Labyrinth," *CiberLetras,* no. 17 (July 2007), n.p.; "Breton et les faux-monnayeurs," *Mélusine: Cahiers du Centre de Recherche sur le Surréalisme* 26 (2006), 223–28; and "The Poetics of Flight: Futurist 'Aeropoesia,'" *MLN* 121, no. 1 (January 2006), 207–24.

Reading Visual Poetry

1
The Word Made Flesh

VISUAL POETRY CAN BE DEFINED BASICALLY AS POETRY THAT IS MEANT to be seen. Although it assumes a great many forms, it inevitably possesses a pictorial as well as a verbal aspect. Combining poetry and painting, the genre presupposes a viewer as well as a reader. How a composition looks, therefore, is as important as what it says. Words no longer serve as simple notational devices but as building blocks in a visual edifice. Known to the Greeks as *technopaigneia* and to the Romans as *carmina figurata,* visual poetry possesses a lengthy and fascinating history. From the very beginning, it appealed to religious and philosophical poets in particular. During the Renaissance the genre experienced a widespread revival, but it was largely neglected thereafter until the beginning of the twentieth century, when it experienced a dramatic rebirth. Intrigued by its seemingly endless possibilities, poets and painters have experimented with visual poetry ever since. Without pretending to provide an exhaustive survey, the present study examines some of the more significant developments that occurred during the twentieth century.

Like visual poetry, which continues to reinvent itself year after year, criticism of visual poetry has undergone an astonishing transformation during the last three decades. As recently as 1978, for example, an astute critic like François Rigolot could dismiss visual poetry as a frivolous pastime. In an article published in a prominent French journal, he asserted that writers who experiment with formal devices tend either to live during unimaginative periods or to lack imagination themselves.[1] Since I have responded to this accusation elsewhere, which dates from the eighteenth century, there is no need to address it here.[2] Suffice it to say that such a statement would be unthinkable today, at least by a reputable critic. Since 1978, visual poetry has come into its own as a legitimate genre with a long history and respectable theoretical credentials. At least a dozen books have appeared in the last thirty years devoted to the study of this intriguing art form. In addition, visual poetry is currently undergoing an enthusiastic revival. An Internet search turns up more than seventy-seven thousand references to contemporary visual poets all over the world. And for those who lack poetic ability, a website called the Poem Generator is available to create works for them.[3] University credit is available not only for courses about visual poetry but also for courses, like Nick Carbó's at the University of Miami and Mairead Byrne's at the Rhode Island School of Design, on how to create visual poetry. The genre has even acquired its own museum: the Ruth and Marvin Sackner Archive of Concrete and Visual Poetry, which houses more than seventy thousand items.[4] Visual poetry is proliferating at such a rapid rate, in fact, that it is impossible to keep track of all the recent developments.

The explanation for such widespread enthusiasm is not hard to find. We live in a visual society, where instantaneous messages are the norm. Although the written word has not yet become obsolete, it has continually lost ground to visual techniques associated with advertising. "In the billboard culture [of today]," Marjorie Perloff explains, "the 'successful' text is one that combines high-speed communication with maximum information."[5] In other words, the successful text is one that imitates art to the best of its ability. Since verbal communication is sequential, however, it is impossible to bridge the gap separating the two modes of expression. The best that literature can do is to reduce that gap by enlisting art on its behalf. The most successful strategy is to create a symbiotic relationship between word and image. By acquiring some artistic traits, visual poetry satisfies our hunger both for visual and for verbal knowledge. As the biblical metaphor in my subtitle suggests, the word in effect becomes flesh. The linguistic skeleton acquires a palpable presence that exerts an immediate effect on the viewer. In contrast to the written (or spoken) message, this effect is direct, instantaneous, and unmediated.

Not surprisingly, since visual poetry represents a hybrid genre, it embraces a great many styles. Certain compositions, like Goy de Silva's "Silencio" (see chapter 2), are almost completely verbal. Except for a cruciform pattern that suddenly appears, the poem is unremarkable. Other compositions, such as Alberto Hidalgo's "Jaqueca" (see chapter 3), are almost exclusively visual. Although the poem is composed wholly of letters, their value is purely decorative. A few works, none of which are examined here, contain no verbal elements whatsoever. This describes the Brazilian Concretist Décio Pignatari's experiments with "semiotic poems," for example, which rely entirely on visual sign systems. Abandoning the linguistic realm, the concept of visual poetry becomes problematic at this point and serves primarily as a metaphor. While some works resemble conventional poems and others resemble paintings or drawings, most fall somewhere between these two extremes.

Although there are some notable exceptions (see chapter 6), reading a visual poem usually involves three distinct operations. The first thing one perceives is the composition's design, which may either be simple or complex, difficult to make out or easily recognizable. While the image imprints itself on the retina instantaneously, it takes a certain amount of time to interpret the image. Perception is not a passive experience, Rudolf Arnheim explains, but a highly active process.[6] In order to recognize a particular shape, the observer must grasp its most important structural features and compare them to a catalogue of perceptual constants. At this stage, therefore, the reader simply functions as a viewer. Before trying to decipher the written text, he or she needs to absorb as much visual information as possible. As Arnheim remarks, "Perceiving accomplishes at the sensory level what in the realm of reasoning is known as understanding." While most visual knowledge is acquired consciously, unconscious cues are often useful as well. For this reason, one needs to be aware of the image's gestalt, which may play an unsuspected role in the poem. Although it appears initially to be insignificant, the long, thin shape of Ignazio Scurto's poem turns out to be important (see chapter 5). The same observation applies to the aerial views in both of Tullio Crali's poems, where the placement of certain words is dictated by topographical features on the ground. "A picture," W. J. T. Mitchell observes, "is a very peculiar and paradoxical creature, both concrete and abstract, both a specific individual thing and a symbolic form that embraces a totality."[7] This amazing complexity is precisely what makes visual imagery so interesting to analyze. Indeed, there sometimes seem to be as many approaches as there are critics. Mitchell suggests that visual images function either as idols, fetishes, or totems.[8] Arnheim prefers to divide them into pictures, symbols, and signs.[9] Visual poetry contains many images that can be analyzed according to these criteria and others that, since they are nonrepresentational, respond better to other approaches.

Once the viewer has contemplated the visual design, the next step is to decipher the text, which shares some of the characteristics Mitchell attributes to pictures. Like visual images, poetic texts are peculiar and paradoxical creatures. The individuals, objects, and actions they name inhabit the poem and yet lie outside it at the same time. They exist both as words and as imaginary creations. Despite our impression of reality, the scene evoked in the poem is situated elsewhere, in an imaginary space engendered by the written text. Like a reflection in the mirror, we can see it and even modify it to some degree, but we cannot actually touch it. In this respect, to be sure, the text of a visual poem is no different than any other poetic text. Where it differs is in its disposition on the page and in the amount of effort required to decipher it. Turning the page this way and that, readers must perform a series of gyrations in order to arrive at their destination. Even poems that have a linear structure are likely to change course at any moment. At the purely verbal level, the mind proceeds cumulatively, holding the words in suspension while ordering and reordering them in a continual search for meaning. Not until the conclusion do the various elements in the poem—visual as well as verbal—coalesce to provide a consistent interpretation.

Before the reader can begin to process the text, however, he or she needs to devise a consistent reading strategy. The text may proceed from left to right and from top to bottom, for example, or it may advance in some other direction. Since there is no hard and fast rule, the reader must necessarily resort to trial and error. Sometimes, when the text is divided into parallel columns, the normal reading model is reversed. One reads from top to bottom initially and only then from left to right. However, visual poetry is not always organized according to literary conventions. As we will discover, many poems follow an artistic model instead. The reader responds to a series of visual cues, which tell him or her how to proceed. The starting point may be marked by a letter that is larger than the others or printed in boldface type (or both). Circular forms typically require one to read in a clockwise direction. Explosive forms radiate out from the center toward the circumference. The list goes on and on. Although one path usually proves to be more rewarding than the others, there are numerous exceptions to this rule. Some Concrete poems, for example, may be approached from multiple angles. Readers can begin anywhere they want and proceed in any direction (see chapter 6). Sometimes a competition exists between literary and artistic strategies, which seem equally attractive. At other times there is a conflict between the two models, each of which violates principles that govern the other. In either case, one must carefully choose between them in order to proceed. More commonly, as we will discover, visual and verbal cues work together to guide the reader through the intersemiotic maze.

The third step requires readers to synthesize the information that has been acquired from the two previous operations. What makes visual poetry so unique, after all, is the way in which the text and the design interact with each other. Reevaluating each one in the light of the other frequently reveals new connections between them. At the very least, it allows the reader to formulate a comprehensive interpretation. However, new insights often occur at this point that have an important bearing on the poem. In many cases, they prompt readers to modify an earlier interpretation. That Vicente Huidobro's "Paysage" evokes a painted canvas, for example, only emerges toward the end of the poem (see chapter 2). That the final section of "Espantapájaros" chronicles Oliverio Girondo's search for certainty becomes clear only upon reflection (see chapter 3). From time to time, an insight is so powerful that it persuades the reader to completely change his or her mind. Someone who believes André Breton is attacking visual poetry in "Pièce fausse," for instance, may suddenly realize (as I did) that he is aiming at another target entirely (see chapter 4).

Although the chapters are arranged chronologically, the following study is not meant to be a literary history. While I have tried to recreate the historical and cultural context surrounding each of the visual poems, the book was conceived primarily as a series of readings. Or more precisely, it was conceived as a series of readings about reading. On the one hand, it seeks to interpret the poems in question, which, despite their apparent simplicity, can be difficult to decipher. On the other hand, it examines the process of interpretation itself, which, like the compositions, can be surprisingly complex. In addition to explicating individual works, therefore, the volume investigates the dynamics involved in reading visual poetry. In the process, it discusses some of the approaches I have found to be the most fruitful over the years. The first chapter considers visual poetry in Spain following the First World War. Introduced by the Chilean poet Vicente Huidobro, who was familiar with the latest French experiments, it appealed to members of the Ultraist movement in particular. The second chapter follows visual poetry to Mexico, where it interested the Estridentistas and members of the Contemporáneos group, and to Argentina, where it attracted the attention of Alberto Hidalgo and Oliverio Girondo. The third chapter examines a number of experiments by Apollinaire's literary heirs in France. Although Tristan Tzara makes a brief appearance, the chapter focuses primarily on André Breton and Pierre Albert-Birot. The next two chapters explore the Futurists' experiments with aeropoetry, which preoccupied them during the 1930s and early 1940s, and retrace the evolution of Concrete poetry in Brazil. In contrast to the Italian poetry, which is virtually unknown, the Brazilian compositions have received worldwide recognition. The final chapter attempts to provide insights into contemporary experiments with digital poetry. Devoted to the Brazilian-American poet Eduardo Kac, it illustrates some of the fascinating options available to poets seeking to exploit recent technological developments.

2
Spanish Ultraist Poetry

UNDER THE GUIDANCE OF RAFAEL CANSINOS-ASSÉNS AND GUILLermo de Torre, the Ultraist movement in Spain flourished from 1919 to 1923. Ironically, what distinguished it from all the other avant-garde movements was the lack of a specific focus. "En nuestro credo cabrán todas las tendencias sin distinción," the *ultraístas* proclaimed in their first manifesto, "con tal que expresen un anhelo nuevo" ["Our credo will include all the different trends, provided that they express a yearning for the new"]. Although the cultivation of novelty and the creation of striking metaphors played a large role in the movement, its dominant characteristic was its unparalleled eclecticism. In their eager search for new principles to replace the *modernista* aesthetic of the previous century, the Ultraists borrowed from everyone around them.

VICENTE HUIDOBRO

As many critics have observed, the Chilean author Vicente Huidobro decisively influenced the development of Spanish Ultraism. Arriving in the Iberian capital in July 1918, where he spent the next five months, Huidobro exhorted the young poets to abandon traditional forms and to embrace an exciting new aesthetic. "His arrival in Madrid," Cansinos later recalled, "was the sole literary event of the year, because he brought with him the latest aesthetic tendencies from abroad."[1] In particular, Huidobro urged his fellow poets to emulate the French poets, who were experimenting with something called "literary cubism." Since he had spent the previous year in Paris, where he published a volume of cubist poetry himself, he spoke with considerable authority. In addition, Huidobro brought numerous examples of the new poetry with him. Since he intended to return to Chile, he had purchased every avant-garde book he could get his hands on. "In his house," Guillermo de Torre later confided,

"I saw the first books and journals of movements that would eventually produce such prodigious and controversial harvests."[2]

Sandwiched in among the French books were copies of Huidobro's latest volume of poetry, entitled *Horizon carré* (*Square Horizon*). In general, René de Costa observes, the French poets who served as Huidobro's models respected the linear character of written discourse. "The typographical innovations," he continues, "are limited to the occasional displacement of margins, the incorporation of large white spaces, and the opportune use of capital letters."[3] This describes most of the poems in *Horizon carré* as well. Although most of the visual effects are unremarkable, one composition exploits pictorial conventions in a spectacular fashion. Dedicated to Pablo Picasso, "Paysage" ("Landscape") juxtaposes five separate pictograms to create a verbo-visual painting. The latter depicts a moonlit scene consisting of a grassy meadow, a huge mountain, a cascading river, a tall tree, and the moon itself. Compared to subsequent experiments by other poets, the typographical effects seem crude and relatively inexpressive. The poem is composed entirely of capital letters except for the image of the moon, whose graceful outline is rendered in lower case letters. Through ignorance or inadvertence, the (silent) *s* in "regardes" was originally omitted. The six remaining phrases utilize two different fonts as building blocks. The larger capitals, which connote solidity and weight, make up the tree, the meadow, and the mountain. The smaller capitals are reserved for more fluid objects such as the song and the river. Except for the moon, which is immediately recognizable, the visual images are far from realistic. The tree reminds one of a massive chess piece, the mountain looks like an Aztec pyramid, and the river resembles a floating staircase. Like the visual analogies cultivated by the Italian Futurists, the images are essentially schematic. Eventually, after repeated scrutiny, one realizes that the visual effects are deliberate rather than accidental. Huidobro is not interested in creating realistic portraits of the objects but rather, like Picasso before him, in reducing them to their geometric equivalents. Looming over the entire collection, the book's title, *Horizon carré,* establishes the basic paradigm at the very beginning. Like the horizon, which is normally circular (360 degrees), the objects in the poem have been modified to conform to Cubist aesthetics.

Surprisingly, for a poem that doubles as a painting, "Paysage" is structured according to verbal conventions. Despite its radical premises, which privilege visual images over linguistic constructions, it adheres to the traditional model. By shifting the poem's title to the left, where it

À PABLO PICASSO

PAYSAGE

LE SOIR ON SE PROMÈNERA SUR DES ROUTES PARALLÈLES

L'ARBRE
ÉTAIT
PLUS
HAUT
QUE LA
MONTAGNE

MAIS LA
MONTAGNE
ÉTAIT SI LARGE
QU'ELLE DÉPASSAIT
LES EXTRÊMITÉS
DE LA TERRE

LE
FLEUVE
QUI
COULE
NE
PORTE
PAS
DE
POISSONS

ATTENTION A NE PAS
JOUER SUR L'HERBE
FRAICHEMENT PEINTE

UNE CHANSON CONDUIT LES BREBIS VERS L'ÉTABLE

1. Vicente Huidobro, “Paysage”

marks the starting point, Huidobro explicitly recognizes this fact. As in traditional poetry, the reader begins at the upper left-hand corner and descends the page line by line. Like a professional typist (or a person eating an ear of corn), one continues from left to right, within the confines of the individual figures, until one reaches the bottom of the page. This strategy is so firmly established that it even governs the decipherment of the moon. Instead of proceeding smoothly in a clockwise direction, as visual conventions would dictate, the reader divides the phrase into three horizontal lines: "La lune / où / tu te regardes." The process described above yields the following poem:

LANDSCAPE
IN THE EVENING WE WILL STROLL DOWN PARALLEL PATHS
The moon in which you look at yourself
THE TREE WAS HIGHER THAN THE MOUNTAIN
BUT THE MOUNTAIN WAS SO WIDE IT PROJECTED
BEYOND THE EARTH'S EDGES
THE FLOWING RIVER CONTAINS NO FISH
DO NOT PLAY ON THE FRESHLY PAINTED GRASS
A SONG LEADS THE SHEEP TOWARD THE STABLE

The first thing one notices is that the poem depends primarily on its visual dimension for its sense. It is not a description of a particular scene so much as a presentation of the scene itself. At the same time, since the latter is highly stylized, the reader remains continually aware of its verbal foundation. Indeed, several images cannot be identified without resorting to verbal clues. Only the moon and the river are readily apparent. Working his or her way through the text, the reader discovers what seems to be a typical pastoral scene. Bathed in moonlight, two lovers stroll side by side, enjoying the natural setting around them. Paralleling their path, a shepherd sings to himself in the distance as he leads his flock home for the night. These details allow us to situate the poem fairly precisely. The scene takes place somewhere in the countryside either at dusk or in the early evening. The reason the tree is higher than the mountain seems to be because it is growing on top of it. This detail is more apparent in a later version of the poem, published in the *Dada Almanach* three years later, in which the tree is positioned directly above the mountain.[4] That the latter is so absurdly wide simply indicates that it blocks a large part of the speaker's view. Suspended high overhead, the moon contains a double (implicit) metaphor. On the one hand, Huidobro compares the bright disc to a circular mirror; on the other, to the face of the speaker's sweetheart reflected in the mirror. Like the heavenly orb, her beautiful countenance is positively radiant. However, the theme of the reciprocal gaze also operates on another level. For as the woman looks at the moon, the moon unexpectedly looks back at her. Huidobro saves a single word for the center of the circle, where it represents the pupil of an enormous eyeball looking down at us.[5]

The two concluding images interrupt the previous reverie and introduce a discordant note. For some reason, the river cascading down the mountainside does not contain any fish—perhaps it is too polluted, or perhaps they have all been caught. In addition, the meadow in the foreground turns out to be completely illusory. Close inspection reveals that what looks like grass is actually green paint. At this point, we perceive we are looking not at a natural scene but at an artistic rendering of a natural scene. The reason the river is devoid of fish, one realizes, is because it is not a real river. Like the elusive meadow, it is an artistic creation. "Paysage" depicts a landscape, all right, but it depicts a landscape *painting*. The horizontal lines at the top and bottom represent the edges of the picture, which in the *Dada Almanach* is signed at the bottom. Huidobro has chosen to exploit the title's ambiguity in order to explore and contrast different modes of representation. The composition consists essentially of a verbal pun that has been raised to the visual level. Instead of a picture poem, it proves to be a picture-of-a-picture poem. Instead of a poem that functions as a painting, it proves to be a poem that functions as a painting of a painting. Like Apollinaire's poem of the same name, on which it is partially modeled, "Paysage" creates a deliberate confusion between illusion and reality.[6] The alternation between three different tenses (another cubist trait) adds to this confusion and emphasizes the work's virtual dimension. Suspended between the past, the present, and the future, "Paysage" occupies an existential limbo.

Huidobro arrived in Spain at precisely the right time, when *modernista* poetry was losing its appeal and poets were looking for other models to emulate. Like other poems in *Horizon carré*, "Paysage" inspired a number of similar works. One of the more interesting examples was published by Adriano del Valle in *Grecia* on December 20, 1919. Entitled "Signo celeste" ("Celestial Sign"), it included two familiar pictograms: a circle and a diagonal zigzag descending from top to bottom.[7] Although he transformed Huidobro's river into a golden staircase and his moon into a whirling spindle, the visual images in both poems are identical—they are simply inverted. Like the circular pictogram in "Paysage," Valle's circle seems to represent the moon as well, which figures prominently in both poems. To be sure, "Paysage" and "Signo celeste" draw on radically different experiences. Valle's composition was inspired not by Cubist painting but by the approaching Christmas season. Despite their obvious verbal differences, however, the poems share a common visual language that each exploits to its own advantage.

JUAN BAUTISTA

"Signo celeste" was the last true visual poem to be created by the Ultraists. A second composition inspired by the same Christmas holiday was little more than a schematic diagram. Entitled "Revelación," it appeared in *Grecia* on December 31, 1919. Composed by Juan Bautista, the poem comprises a religious meditation interspersed with prayer and depicts God's all-seeing eye. Visually it consists of an equilateral triangle inscribed in a circle, from which four diagonals radiate in different directions. The circle itself reproduces the first half of the Lord's Prayer. Enclosing the word "**DIOS**" ["**GOD**"] in large boldface capitals, the triangle reads as follows: "solo tales elementos pudieron engendrar un **DIOS** que simultaneamente fuese CEREBRAL Y—¡OH MAGDALENA!—MEDULAR" ["only these elements could engender a **GOD** who is both CEREBRAL AND—OH MARY MAGDALEN!—MEDULLARY."] The elements in question appear to be the Father, the Son, and the Holy Spirit—symbolized by the equilateral triangle—whose names adorn the figure's three corners. The four groups of radiating lines divide the twelve apostles, according to Bautista's bizarre distinction, into either cerebral or medullary personalities.

In contrast to the cerebrum, which is concerned with perception, thought, and conscious impulses, the medulla oblongata controls the body's autonomic nervous system. Bautista seems to be referring to the division between mind and body, between thought and passion, that has informed Western metaphysics since the beginning. Thus the cerebral apostles—Paul, Peter, and John—are opposed to the intuitive apostles—Lebbeus, James the son of Alphaeus, and Simon. And those who are not very cerebral—Bartholomew, Thomas, and Philip—are opposed to those who are not very intuitive—Andrew, Matthew, and James the son of Zebedee. As a former prostitute, Mary Magdalen is naturally associated with the body and its various functions. Ironically, since the Virgin Mary was primarily the receptacle of the divine impulse, she belongs to a similar category ("minimum cerebrality"). Where Bautista's taxon-

REVELACIÓN

¡¡¡HOSANNA!!!...

—¡OH MAGDALENA!—

MEDULAR

2. Juan Bautista, "Revelación"

omy breaks down, he finally informs us, is where the Creator is concerned. Just as God somehow manages to combine three identities in one, He alone is able to abolish the traditional mind/body dichotomy.

Isaac del Vando-Villar

Isaac del Vando-Villar published a similar schematic poem in *Grecia* on October 30, 1919, entitled "En el infierno de una noche" ("In the Inferno of a Night"). Cast in the shape of a cross, it appears at first glance to embody a religious theme like "Revelación." This impression is reinforced by the reference to Hell in the title and by the diagonal shafts of light radiating out from the cross's center. Unlike the works examined previously, the poem is composed largely of outlined forms. Indeed, its forcefulness derives almost entirely from the heavy, dark outlines that enclose much of the text, which itself is written in large, boldface letters. Once again, one expects to encounter a passionate statement of religious faith —stemming perhaps from the tumultuous night in question. However, this impression is dispelled as soon as one begins to read the text. Enclosed by the topmost crossbar, the largest word marks the poem's starting point and provides a convenient subtitle. Descending the page syllable by syllable and word by word, the reader deciphers the cross's vertical post, its horizontal crossbar, and the box at the bottom on which it is presumably resting. Next, he or she turns the page forty-five degrees to the left to read the first group of diagonal lines and forty-five degrees to the right to read the second group. This procedure generates the following poem:

KURSAAL
THE SWALLOWS KNOW ALL THE SECRETS
OF OUR POCKETBOOKS
NO ONE KNOWS WHAT
CAN HAPPEN TO HIM
ON THAT NIGHT, NO ONE . . .
THE WAITERS ARE DRESSED / IN MOURNING FOR US / THEIR VICTIMS.
THE VIOLINISTS SEEM / SOAKING WET BENEATH / THEIR BOWS' WHITE SPURTS.
THE PASSING BOOTBLACKS / POLISH OUR / SHOES WITH THEIR GLANCES.
A BLACK MAN / HAS SHOT A CHAMPAGNE ROCKET / INTO THE AIR.

Unfortunately, reducing the original poem to a linear format fails to make it any more intelligible. While titles are traditionally supposed to

En el Infierno de una Noche

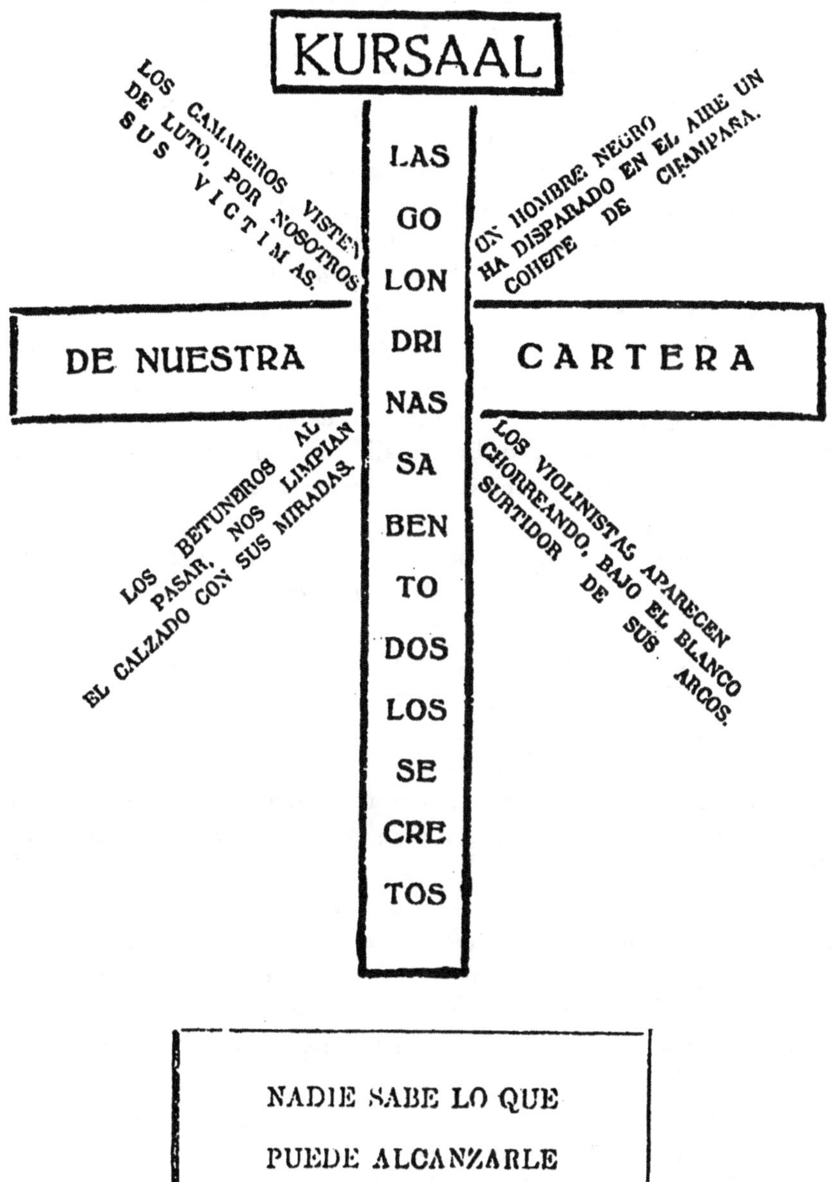

KURSAAL

LOS CAMAREROS VISTEN DE LUTO, POR NOSOTROS SUS VICTIMAS.

UN HOMBRE NEGRO HA DISPARADO EN EL AIRE UN COHETE DE CHAMPAÑA.

LAS
GO
LON
DRI
NAS
SA
BEN
TO
DOS
LOS
SE
CRE
TOS

DE NUESTRA CARTERA

LOS BETUNEROS AL PASAR, NOS LIMPIAN EL CALZADO CON SUS MIRADAS.

LOS VIOLINISTAS APARECEN CHORREANDO, BAJO EL BLANCO SURTIDOR DE SUS ARCOS.

NADIE SABE LO QUE
PUEDE ALCANZARLE
EN ESA NOCHE, NADIE...

3. Isaac del Vando-Vilar, "En el inferno"

introduce the work in question, the present title is thoroughly enigmatic. Which night is the poet talking about, one wonders, and why does he call it an inferno? Hoping to discover a clue that will shed some light on these questions, one turns to the subtitle, which proves equally uninformative. The word "kursaal" is so obscure that one needs a multivolume reference work to locate it. The *New Century Dictionary* provides the following definition: "A public building or room for the use of visitors at a health resort in Germany or elsewhere." Apparently this is not a religious poem after all. Although the *New Century* definition is doubtless historically accurate, it does not tell the whole story. Despite the word's apparent rarity, an Internet search turns up two hundred eighty thousand references! Unexpectedly, the word "kursaal" turns out to be surprisingly common. Indeed, so many hotels, restaurants, and casinos have incorporated it into their name that it has become synonymous with luxury. According to all indications, the poem appears to be situated not in a church or in a German spa but in a hotel dining room.

Although we do not know exactly where the Hotel Kursaal is located, it seems to be fairly luxurious like its numerous namesakes. The waiters are dressed in tuxedos, bootblacks are available for guests to patronize, and a string quartet is playing quietly in a corner. In addition, it appears to be a gala evening of some sort—very possibly New Year's Eve. We already know it is a special night, and one of the waiters has just uncorked a bottle of champagne, perhaps in preparation for midnight. Unlike the rest of the people in the room, who are in a celebratory mood, Vando-Villar does not seem to be having a very good time. The picture he paints of the gathering is not just jaundiced but positively gloomy. Beneath a sprinkling of lighthearted metaphors involving rockets and jets of water, a darker portrait emerges. The waiters are dressed in funereal black. The people in the room are depicted as victims rather than guests. The violinists are not just dripping wet (*chorreando*) but are complaining (*choreando*). Even the passing bootblacks seem unduly critical. The last straw is provided by the "golondrinas," who are not swallows after all but pickpockets who have managed to insinuate themselves into the crowd. Swooping down on their unsuspecting prey, they surreptitiously relieve them of their valuables. As the poet proclaims in the title, the experience certainly seems like pure Hell. Whether his description is objective or purely imaginary is difficult to say. In the last analysis, it makes little difference—all that matters is that Vando-Villar is miserable.

Pedro Raida

On November 20, 1919, Pedro Raida published a more substantial visual poem in *Grecia* entitled "EL FUTURO NIDO" ("THE FUTURE NEST"). Although the Ultraists generally disdained solid forms, Raida used them exclusively in his visual poetry. Piling four or five blocks of text on top of each other, he created an imposing structure resembling a step pyramid. Next, with the help of half a dozen linear phrases, he added four walls and a roof to create a primitive house. Since each block is smaller than the one below it, the finished building looks more like a wedding cake than an actual residence. The fact that the picture supposedly depicts a villa does not alter the viewer's initial impression. Since "EL FUTURO NIDO" was conceived as a (visual) poem in prose, it tends to observe normal reading conventions. Apart from a few unorthodox excursions, the composition reads from left to right and from top to bottom. The chief exceptions are the walls and the roof, which need to be processed separately. Whereas the right side of the roof reads from top to bottom, the left side reads from bottom to top. Forced to choose between verbal and visual conventions—between legibility and visibility—Raida chose the only viable solution. By contrast, the four walls read from left to right and from top to bottom (in two stages), but they privilege the latter operation over the former. While the roof reverses the normal reading direction, the walls reverse the normal reading sequence.

THE
FUTURE
NEST.

AZURE VILLA IS MY CHALET.

I
don't have it yet.
I dream of possessing it.
I
will build it
save error or oversight.

I AM HE WHO
SAID NO MORE YESTERDAY

AZURE VILLA
will avoid the vain splendor of stone without succumbing to the ostentation of marble.
AZURE VILLA
supreme jewel of simplicity and elegance, luxuriant and concise, possessing a single floor

VILLA AZUL ES MI CHALET.

aún
no lo tengo.
Sueño con poseerlo.
Lo
edificaré
y salvo error u omisión.

YO SOY AQUEL

VILLA AZUL
esquivará el fausto de la piedra sin propender a la ostentación del mármol.

VILLA AZUL
suprema gala de sencillez y elegancia, ubérrima y breve, de una sola planta y un resplandor único, reverberará en la gracia de Atenas sobre la encarnación del severismo y la dureza romana; por cuanto el temperamento de villa azul abaluartará el Evangelio de Cristo, trajeándose del bello sensualismo del paisaje andaluz.

QUE AYER NO MAS DECIA

VILLA AZUL
acampará por sus muros, nubes de campanillas azules, emergidas de lechos jazminados entre rosas y en tropel de frondas y músicas, violadas por los pinceles del monóculo universal.

Altos pinos, palmeras volubles
atraerán las chispas de los radiogramas que lanzan las aves en la mañana azul y el mediodía azul y la tarde azul. Los esposos, beberemos en el vaso de sol, la copa del aire, el ánfora de la luna y el cáliz de las estrellas todo el germen de la hermosura ultraista, semejante a un vino de pasiones sangradas en primavera. Los esposos emular quieren a las aves sedientas de luz y de espacio, de árboles y flores, de la tierra y la fuente, que sólo aspiran a un nido entre lujuriosa vegetación, para huir del frio de la noche oscura y buscar el lecho cálido que los refundiera en un solo amor,

Mientras nacen la piedra y la arena, el ladrillo y la cal, el agua y el bosque que constituyan el organismo de:

VILLA AZUL...,

Pedro Raida.

4. Pedro Raida, "Futuro nido"

and a unique brilliance, will incarnate Athens's
grace rather than Roman harshness and severity;
since azure villa's character will fortify the
Gospel of Christ, clothing itself in the beautiful
sensuality of the Andalusian landscape.

AZURE VILLA

swarms of bluebells will camp by its walls, sprung from jasmine
beds among roses and in a jumble of fronds and tunes, violated by
the paintbrushes of the universal monocle.

Tall Pines, Voluble Palms

will attract the radiograms' sparks that the birds send in the azure morning and the azure midday and the azure afternoon. From the sun's glass, the air's cup, the moon's amphora, and the stars' calyx, husbands and wives will drink the essence of Ultraist beauty, like the wine of bloody passion in the springtime. They will imitate the birds, who thirst for light and space, for trees and flowers, for the earth and water, who only aspire to nest among luxurious vegetation, to flee the dark night's chill, and to find a warm bed that will recast them in a single love.

Meanwhile the stone and sand, the brick and lime, the water and forest are being created that will constitute the organism of:

AZURE VILLA. . . .

Although the poem requires the reader to pay close attention, a cursory reading suffices to reveal several interesting facts. The most important discovery is that "EL FUTURO NIDO" is a devotional poem. The "nest" in the title is a metaphor for Raida's future abode in heaven where, as a pious Christian, he hopes to go after he dies. At the same time it is also a metaphor for the Villa Azul, which serves as the dominant metaphor for Raida's celestial dwelling. Among other things, the composition's devotional aspect explains the building's curious architecture. The reason the building is blue, it turns out, is because it is located in the sky. Despite the poet's repeated claims that it represents a villa, moreover, the picture clearly portrays a church. Doubling as the poem's title, the cross at the top confirms the building's identity. This encourages us to reexamine another curious feature: the vertical phrases, which in retrospect do not seem to represent walls at all. The fact that they are enclosed by heavy, dark crochets is puzzling, to say the least. What could possibly be their function? In theory, the mysterious features could conceivably represent flying buttresses. However, a quick review of Gothic architecture reveals that they are niches harboring religious statues.

While Spanish churches come in different styles, one of the more popular models features two niches on both sides of the entrance, one above the other—exactly as they appear here.

The verbal composition itself belongs to a lengthy tradition of mystical poetry dating back to the Middle Ages and before. While mysticism has always played a significant role in Spanish literature, it combines with a secular, Utopian vision in "EL FUTURO NIDO" to depict an ideal existence unsullied by human contingencies. The leading authority on Ultraism, Gloria Videla, dismisses Raida with the comment, "He did not possess poetic gifts."[8] Although there is much in this poem to support her claim, the composition possesses a certain interest of its own. Raida confides initially that the edifice he is about to describe is only a dream. While he speaks of constructing it himself, this is simply a metaphor—albeit one that structures the entire poem. What he is actually talking about is earning the right to *inhabit* the Villa Azul—in other words, the right to enter Heaven. Although the building belongs to the Almighty, the construction metaphor creates the impression that God and Raida own it jointly. This impression is reinforced by the introduction, in which the poet clearly identifies with the villa. In particular, we learn the latter is endowed with a number of human virtues, including modesty and humility. Besides Athenian grace, Raida confides, it embodies Christian fortitude and Andalusian sensuality. Eventually it dawns on the reader that the poet is primarily talking about himself. These are the virtues he plans to cultivate in order to convince God to let him inhabit the Villa Azul.

The remainder of the poem describes Raida's vision of celestial paradise, which, like many poets before him, he equates with perpetual springtime. Remarkably, he manages to breathe new life into this ancient literary topos, which has a long and varied history.[9] To be sure, the first three lines are traditional. The villa will be surrounded by countless flowers of every variety, whose extraordinary beauty will provide an unforgettable setting. The fourth line attempts to expand this portrait but unfortunately fails miserably. According to Raida, the flowers will be "violadas por los pinceles del monóculo universal" ["violated by the paintbrushes of the universal monocle"]. The phrase is so awkward and so convoluted that one begins to sympathize with Videla. How can a flower be violated, one wonders, especially by a paintbrush? How can a paintbrush be wielded by a monocle? What on earth makes the monocle universal? The rhetorical jungle seems nearly impenetrable. But little by little, one begins to grasp what Raida is trying to say. The flowers are so beautiful that artists come from all over to paint their picture. Or rather, since the final noun is singular, one artist in particular comes to pay homage to their beauty, an artist wearing a stylish monocle. The reason the monocle is universal, one gradually perceives, is because it belongs to God, who possesses an all-seeing eye. Unexpectedly, the phrase turns out to be blasphemous on two accounts. It is hard to say which is more shocking—the thought of the Almighty violating the flowers or the image of God as a Sunday painter.

By contrast, the remainder of the poem is thoroughly charming. Since the Villa Azul is located in the sky, a blue light suffuses the scene all day long. Otherwise Raida's vision of celestial paradise resembles the earthly paradise described in the Bible. Like the Garden of Eden, it is filled with trees and flowers, grassy meadows, and gurgling streams. Like Eden, it is populated by countless birds and other animals, which live in harmony with mankind and each other. In addition, it is designed exclusively for couples who, like Adam and Eve, will live together in a state of natural grace. Inspired by the Ultraist beauty all around them, husbands and wives will cultivate simple pleasures, concentrate on their basic needs, and devote themselves to each other. The most interesting inhabitants are not the human residents, however, but the marvelous birds, which play a key role in the poem. Since they are Ultraist birds, they send radiotelegrams to each other instead of simply singing. Unfortunately, Raida confuses wireless telegraphy with conventional telegraphy, which utilizes electrical impulses. More importantly, the birds serve as models for the celestial couples, who strive to imitate them. Like their avian companions, they learn to appreciate the simple things in life, including a nice warm bed where they can curl up and be happy.

Visual Analogies

In general, the most important visual experiments in Spain took place between June and December 1919.[10] Only Guillermo de Torre continued to write visual poetry after that date, poetry that culminated in the publication of *Hélices* (*Propellers*) in 1923.[11] Although visual poetry was restricted primarily to the second half of 1919, visual elements continued to appear well into 1921. On January 20, 1920, for example, *Grecia* published another work by Raida whose visual component was extremely rudimentary. "En el seno de los modernos atletas del canto" ("In the Breast of the Modern Athletes of Song") simply zigzags down the page, from one side to the other and back again. As the title suggests, the poem extols modern singers' accomplishments and compares them to trained athletes. The visual design is apparently meant to evoke acrobats swinging from one trapeze to another. However, the schematic representation is difficult to decipher and not particularly convincing. As much as anything, Raida's poem testifies to the demise of visual poetry in Spain. At the same time, it illustrates a popular device that the Ultraists borrowed, like expressive typography, from the Italian Futurists: visual analogy (*analogia disegnata*). The first example was invented in january 1914 by Francesco Cangiullo, who transformed the word "fumare" ("to smoke") into FUUUUUMARE, so that it appeared to expand like a puff of smoke. Goy de Silva employed a similar device in a poem entitled "Silencio," published in *Cervantes* in February 1919, where he juxtaposed the four cardinal points to form a star. Arranging them in the shape of a cross,

```
             N
             O
             R
             T
             E
OESTE               ESTE

             S
             U
             R
```

he bisected each right angle with three lines so that light seemed to be radiating from the center.

Andrés Nimero

By the end of the year, the use of visual analogies had become widespread in Ultraist poetry. Several interesting examples occur in a poem by Andrés Nimero called "Poema alfa de la gran circunvalación" ("Alpha Poem on the Great Circle Route"). Published in *Grecia* on October 12, 1919, the composition consists of some eighty-four lines accompanied by eight visual elements. It recounts a trip in Seville on Streetcar 24 along the Great Circle Route, beginning and ending in the Plaza Nueva (also called the Plaza de San Fernando). Surrounded by hotels and bordered with date palms on all four sides, the latter was the largest square in

POEMA ALFA DE LA GRAN CIRCUNVALACION

0'35 ptas.

Hay coches, caballos, autos... Hotel de gran ciudaD
E

2

L
A
R
G
A
S

F
I
L
A

NIÑOS

SOLDADOS

FALTA EL
MONUMENTO A
SAN FERNANDO

VAGOS

LIMPIABOTAS

P
A
L
M
E
R
A
S

P
O
L
V

SOBRE ESTE LADO ESTA EL AYUNTAMIENTO

SUENA UNA CAMPANA Y RUEDA UN TUMULTO DE HIERRO VIEJO...

El cobrador moja los dedos
y arranca el
billete.
(El cobrador nunca se afeita) y fuma...
Trin... Trin. Tlan, tlon. Marcha el vehículo.
Plaza de la Constitución de San Francisco.
La Audiencia está quemada.
Se ennegreció la Justicia.
Una cocinera manda detener el tranvía
y sube con un gran cesto.
La Catedral.
Por la Plaza
del Triunfo
Pasa
un
cura
con un rojo quitasol.
Rechina la curva

5a. Andrés Nimero, "Poema alfa de la gran circunvalación"

Seville. On summer evenings, people would come from all over to hear the municipal band play. According to contemporary maps, the Great Circle Route was one of six streetcar lines serving the city, five of which departed from this square.[12] Unlike the Pequeña Circunvalación cars, which were decorated with green stripes, or those on the Línea San-Pedro-Calzada, which had blue stripes, the Great Circle cars were emblazoned with a red cross. Whereas the other streetcars left at twenty-minute intervals, the Great Circle cars departed every ten minutes. At the top of the page, Nimero quotes the price of the ticket in large boldface numerals: 0'35 ptas. Immediately below, a rectangular diagram represents the Plaza Nueva, whose four sides read as follows: "Hay coches, caballos, autos . . . Hotel de gran ciudad / DE PALMERAS POLVO / SOBRE ESTE LADO ESTA EL AYUNTAMIENTO / 2 LARGAS FILAS" ["There are carriages, horses, autos . . . Large city hotel / THE PALMS DUST / THE CITY HALL IS ON THIS SIDE / 2 LONG LINES"]. For some reason, probably because he needed more room, Nimero moved the handsome Renaissance city hall from the eastern side of the square to its southern edge. Otherwise, the rectangular diagram is reasonably accurate. The two long lines on the left may represent people waiting for the streetcar or, more likely, the streetcar tracks themselves. The palms on the right may be actual trees or the name of the hotel or both. The "polvo" next to them may be a dusty stretch of pavement or an advertisement for some kind of powder, possibly a medicine or a cosmetic. In the center of the square, which is filled with "NIÑOS, SOLDADOS, LIMPIABOTAS, and VAGOS" ["CHILDREN, SOLDIERS, BOOTBLACKS, and LOAFERS,"] an oval marks the spot where a statue of San Fernando was about to be installed.

Sandwiched between two parallel lines representing tracks, the next sentence evokes the sounds of the streetcar preparing to depart: "SUEÑA UNA CAMPANA Y RUEDA UN TUMULTO DE HIERRO VIEJO . . ." ["A BELL RINGS AMID THE NOISE OF OLD IRON."]. "El cobrador moja los dedos," Nimero adds, "y arranca el / billete. / (El cobrador nunca se afeita) y fuma . . . / Trin . . . Trin. Tlan, tlon. Marcha el vehículo ["The conductor moistens his fingers / and collects the / tickets. / (The conductor never shaves) and smokes . . . / Ding . . . Ding . . . Dong, dong. The vehicle departs." Thereafter the poem records the streetcar's itinerary street by street, monument by monument, until it has covered half the city.

Constitution Square of St. Francis.
The Courthouse burned down.

y la estridencia se va
por el Arco de Mañara
Puerta de Jerez. El Ceibo Sagrado...
(antes de Rebello, fué Sicomoro)
En su copa no está el loro.
La Pasarela es el armazón del Municipio.
Arboles y la Casa de Socorro.
Estamos en la Puerta de la Carne (Piaza Monumental
(Torea Joselito.
La carne adherida al hueso:
Puerta del Osario. Sandías.
Perneo. Laguna. Laboratorio.
La Trinidad: Cárcel de las Santas Patronas.
Fábricas. Por aquí se va a Miraflores.
Ruum... Ruum... Ruum...
Y llegamos a Capuchinos.
Templo de aldea.
¡Ya se quedó atrás el DOLOR
De los tuberculosos!
El dolor persiste sin embargo
Los pobres sin albergue:
Sanchezdalp..
Camino del cementerio.
Hospital civil.
Hospital militar.
(¿Un civil es militar?)
Lejos destila la lepra.
(Coeur de Jeannete)
«Llevaba una mano fuera...»

«Mare mía e la Esperansa...»
(Tambores... Cornetas.
MEDIODÍA DEL VIERNES)
La Feria. No es Jueves.

☐ Hércules ☐

El amor ronda

Por la planicie afrodisiaca y cínica. Cine.
Entre la Avenida del Amor Profano
Y la calle del Amor de Dios

5b. Andrés Nimero, "Poema alfa de la gran circunvalación"

The Palace of Justice was burned black.
A cook signals the streetcar to stop
and climbs aboard carrying a large basket.
The Cathedral.
Through the Triumphal
Square
A
priest
passes
with a red parasol.
Clanking around the bend
the noise disappears
through the Mañara Arch
Jerez Gate. The Sacred Flame Tree . . .
(before Rebello it was a Sycamore)
There are no parrots in its branches.
The Footbridge is the Town's backbone.
Trees and the Emergency Hospital.
We are at Butchers' Gate
    Bullfight Arena
    Joselito is fighting today.
Meat stuck to the bone:
Ossuary Gate. Watermelons.
Perneo. Laguna. Laboratorio.
The Trinity: Patron Saints Prison.
Factories. This way leads to Miraflores.
Ruum . . . Ruum . . . Ruum . . .
And we arrive at Capuchinos.
Rustic church.
The PAIN of the tuberculosis patients
remained behind!
However pain persists
Homeless people:
Sanchezdalp.
The cemetery road.
Civil hospital.
Military hospital.
(Is a civilian a soldier?)
Leprosy files past in the distance.
(*Coeur de Jeanette*)
"Her hand was sticking out . . ."

Running along the northern edge of the Plaza Nueva, the streetcar heads east and enters the Plaza de la Constitución (behind the actual City

Hall). One of the busiest parts of the city, it is surrounded by balconied houses and bordered on the east by the courthouse. As Nimero remarks, the building burned down at the turn of the century but was rebuilt in 1908. Proceeding directly south, the streetcar traverses the Plaza del Triunfo enclosed by the Cathedral, where Christopher Columbus is buried; the Alcázar, the former palace of the Moorish kings; and the Casa Lonja, where the Archivo General de Indias is located. Continuing until it reaches the Mañara Arch and the Jerez Gate, it turns left and proceeds along the Calle San Fernando past the immense two-story tobacco factory—made famous by Bizet's *Carmen*—until it comes to the Pasarela. Turning left again, the streetcar heads north along the ring road in a counterclockwise direction. On the right, it passes the emergency hospital and the gate leading to the slaughterhouse, both of which are mentioned in the poem. The Butchers' Gate reminds Nimero that the famous matador Joselito is fighting in the bull ring on the other side of town. As Spanish custom dictates, the bulls he dispatches will be butchered and the meat given to the poor. Continuing on its way, the streetcar passes the church of La Trinidad and the Capuchin convent, which, as Nimero informs us, resembles a rustic temple. The sight of the Hospital Civil y Militar prompts him to question the wisdom of treating soldiers and civilians under the same roof. It reminds him as well of the poor, the sick, and the homeless who have to beg for a living.

The reference to *Coeur de Jeanette* at this point, a famous French perfume, is somewhat puzzling. It may allude to a store where it was sold, or perhaps to a passenger who is wearing it. Juxtaposed with the mention of leprosy in the preceding line, the reference seems highly ironic. The quotation in the next line was prompted by the road leading to the Cemetery San Fernando, also known as the Bullfighters' Cemetery. It refers to a story by Gustavo Adolfo Bécquer entitled "La Venta de los Gatos" ("The Cat Market"), situated in a dance hall of this name in the very same quarter. Recalling his sweetheart's burial in the San Fernando cemetery, the protagonist exclaims:

En el carro de los muertos
ha pasado por aquí;
llevaba una mano fuera,
por ella la conocí

[In the carriage of the dead
she passed by here;
her hand was sticking out,
that's how I knew her.][13]

Arriving at the Macarena Gate, which marks the northernmost point of the journey, the streetcar's passengers encounter another visual analogy: "ARCO DE LA MACARENA," which is rounded like the top of the gate itself. Beneath the arch is an arrow pointing to the left accompanied by the words "una saeta" ("an arrow"). This verbo-visual doubling repeats that of the arch and points to an underlying pun: "arco" means both "arch" and "bow." Although the pun is initiated verbally, it is most effective at the visual level where, the image suggests not only an arch but a bow shooting an arrow into the distance. Turning left at this point, the streetcar heads directly south.

"Mare mía e la Esperanza . . ."
(Drums . . . Bugles.)
(MIDDAY FRIDAY)
The Fair. It's not Thursday.

☐ Hércules ☐

Love Circle
Across the aphrodisiacal and cynical plateau. Cinema.
Between the Avenue of Profane Love
And the Love of God Street
EUROPE
Here were:
Barrera
Varieties
Friends of Art
Realito
All, all gone up in flames.

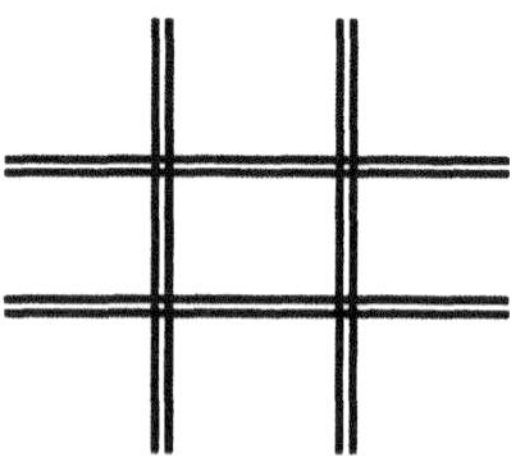

Novedades suffers from old age
The Small Bell and the Great Bell.
Caramels and toys.

Noise The prestige of Sierpes Street

Europa
Aquí fueron:
Barrera
Variedades
Amigos del Arte
Realito
Todo, todo torrefacto.

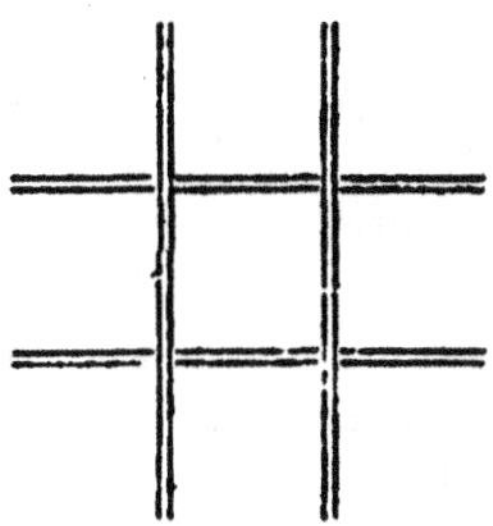

La vejez de Novedades
La Campanilla y la Campana.
Caramelos y juguetes.

Ruido El prestigio de calle Sierpes

Sujeta esquinas. Tránsito ininterrumpido.
La Fiambrera.
Comestibles.
Málaga. A las 8 hay pescado.
O'Donnell - La Magdalena.
Una triste fuente seca en el Pacífico.
¡The Seville Water Works!
Y vamos por Méndez Núñez..
Hotel. Hostal. Fonda. Hospedería.
Novios de moro.
The Berlitz School.
El Arte ha roto la monotonía.
De la contrata.
PLAZA NUEVA. San Fernando.
Se ha completado el ciclo.
Llegada. Es de noche.
El tranvía. - Minotauro número **24**

Enciende su ojo rojo
Y busca otra vez el camino.

Andrés NIMERO

5c. Andrés Nimero, "Poema alfa de la gran circunvalación"

Corners. Smooth sailing.
The Lunch Box.
Groceries.
Málaga. At 8:00 they have fish.
O'Donnell — La Magdalena.
A sad, dry fountain in the Pacific.
The Seville Water Works!
And we continue along Méndez Núñez.
Hotel. Inn. Tavern. Hostelry.
Moorish newlyweds.
The Berlitz School.
Art has broken the monotony.
Of the contract.
PLAZA NUEVA. San Fernando.
The cycle is complete.
Arrival. Night is falling.

The streetcar. — Minotaur number **24**

Ignites its red eye
And continues on its way.

Amid snatches of an anonymous song, the streetcar descends the Calle de la Feria ("Fair Street") until it encounters the Calle Correduría angling off to the right, leading first to the Plaza de Europa and then to the Alameda de Hércules. In 1574, two Roman columns were erected at the south end, bearing statues of Hercules and Julius Caesar. Momentarily adopting an aerial perspective, Nimero depicts these as two squares on either side of the word "Hércules." Continuing in a southern direction, the streetcar descends the Calle Amor de Diós, which occasions some wordplay about love, crosses the Calle Campana ("Bell Street"), and enters the Calle de las Sierpes. A narrow but extremely fashionable street, the latter originally derived its name from a tavern sign depicting serpents. Like the intersection, which resembles a tic-tac-toe diagram, it is depicted visually. Amor de Diós and Sierpes streets were lined with shops, cafes, and clubs, which Nimero evokes in considerable detail. Although many of them were relatively new, the venerable Cafe de Novedades — whose name belied its age — was still there. At the end of the first block, the streetcar turns right onto the Calle O'Donnell and then left into the Plaza del Pacifíco where, ironically, there is not enough water to power the fountain. Offering a brief glimpse of the splendid Santa Maria Magdalena church, it continues south on the Calle Méndez

Núñez until it returns to the Plaza Nueva, where it pauses to unload passengers and pick up new ones. As night begins to fall, Streetcar 24 acquires an unexpected mythological dimension. Surrounded by a jumble of labyrinthine streets, it resembles the legendary Minotaur ensconced in his famous maze. Equipped with a single headlight, it disappears into the darkness like a mechanical Cyclops in search of wily Odysseus.

More Visual Analogies

A particularly amusing visual analogy occurrs in a poem entitled "El aviador Dada" ("The Dada Aviator"), published in *Grecia* on January 20, 1920, in which the author fantasizes about intervening in the Russian Revolution disguised as a fly. Composed by Jacques Edwards, a Chilean living in Paris, the poem was originally written in French. Half way through his humorous monologue, one suddenly encounters the word *mosca* ("fly") scattered all over the page. Unexpectedly, the insect seems to be madly dancing about the sheet of paper. Ramón Alvarez Serrano utilized a different device in another whimsical fly poem entitled "La preconsulta del Dr. Wollman" ("Dr. Wollman's Preliminary Consultation"). Appearing in *Grecia* on February 20, 1920, it recounts the story of a fly which, daring to disturb the peace of a treatise on obstetrics, is driven away by a flask of nitric acid. As the poem begins, the treatise is lying open on the table, and its letters are playing ring-around-the-rosy in the middle of the page. Set off from the body of the text, the phrase "COGIDITAS DE LA MANO" ("HAND-IN-HAND") is twisted into a spiral to suggest their circular movement.

The same issue of *Grecia* included a rather macabre composition by Rogelio Buendía entitled "Rayos X" ("X Rays"). Although the title suggests it is concerned with radiology, the action takes place in an emergency ward, where a man is experiencing a heart attack. The gravity of the situation, which is described in great detail, and the poem's hallucinatory imagery create an atmosphere of almost unbearable intensity. Presented as a dramatic monologue, the poem traces the man's sensations from the beginning to the end of the attack, as the doctors work feverishly to save him. The whole scene is bathed in an eerie half-light—described as "luz color de manzana" ("apple-colored light")—which causes the poet to compare it to an underwater grotto. Without the poem's visual component, however, the drama would be completely incomprehensible. Neither its subject nor its setting nor its conclusion would make any sense. Buendía remedies this situation by reproducing the patient's electrocardiogram at different stages of the attack. At first, the machine draws a strong horizontal line with regularly spaced peaks, indicating that his heartbeat has returned to normal. Halfway through the poem, however, the patient's condition worsens, and the cardiogram shows only two peaks. The final cardiogram is completely flat. All we see are the restless stirrings of the mechanical pen as its drags along the page. . . .

Francisco Vighi

It remains to mention two more Ultraist poems that exploit visual devices to good effect. Authored by Francisco Vighi, the first appeared in *Reflector* in December 1920. Entitled "CELESTIALES FUEGOS ARTIFICIALES" ("CELESTIAL FIREWORKS"), it presents an apocalyptic vision of the end of the world.

Ssss.........................Boom!
        The festival began

The lord of the heavens
                plays tricks
                        with bright stars and comets.
The angels discharge their shotguns.

Four firecrackers together
        back! back! back! back!

The Lord sprinkles
the sky with *alpha and omega* stars
        and a litany of stars,
Saint Peter murmurs in the gate house.

Dramatic flashes.
                Later
Saint Mark releases a fiery bull;
the eleven thousand virgins (I like them all)
        and the holy bearded fathers
                are frightened.

        Crash! Bang!
        Saint Christopher
        sneezed twice.

FUEGOS ARTIFICIALES

Fchsss........................ ¡¡Pon!!

C Empezó la función E

El señor de las alturas
hace diabluras
con luceros y cometas.
Los angelitos disparan sus escopetas.

L E S

Cuatro petardos a compás
¡tras! ¡tras! ¡tras! ¡tras!

T I A

El Señor, riega
el cielo de estrellas *alfa* y *omega*
y estrellas de letanía,
San Pedro murmura en la portería.

L E S

Relámpagos teatrales.
Luego
San Marcos suelta un toro de fuego;
se asustan
las oncemil virgenes (todas me gustan)
y los santos padres barbudos.

F U E

¡Cataplún! ¡Cataplón!
dió dos estornudos
San Cristobalón.

G O S

Serpentina de magnesio y latín
a cargo de San Agustín.

A R

Traca española
por el valenciano Vicente Ferrer
y el guipuzcoano Ignacio Loyola.

T I

Santa Bárbara, maestra en el oficio
y su antípoda compañero
Pedro Botero
queman la torre de artificio.

F
I
C
I

A L E S

Un trueno profundo.
Terrible explosión.
Se acabó el mundo.
¡¡¡Pon!!!

6. Francesco Vighi, "Celestiales"

Magnesium and Latin streamers
        supervised by Saint Augustine.

A string of Spanish firecrackers
by Vicente Ferrer from Valencia
and Ignacio Loyola from Guipúzcoa.

Saint Barbara, mistress of the holy office,
and her antipodal companion
                Pedro Botero
set fire to the heap of fireworks.

                A tremendous boom.
                Terrible explosion.
                The world evaporated.
                BANG!!!

The poem itself is divided into ten irregular stanzas comprising between two and four lines each. Short stanzas alternate with long stanzas and vice versa. Although the lines have no fixed length, Vighi goes to considerable pains to make them rhyme. Indeed, he employs at least three distinct rhyme schemes, which he varies as the mood strikes him. Dividing the poem into two parallel columns so that it completely fills the page, he breaks the title into syllables and letters and strews them about the text. Since the title utilizes oversized letters, the fragments have a spatializing effect, breaking the poem into pieces as well and mirroring the celestial fireworks. Some of the fragments are upside down; others are turned sideways, forcing the reader to rotate the page completely to decipher the composition. Although at first glance they appear to be distributed randomly, they preserve their logical order and serve to separate the stanzas.

In theory, all fireworks displays are "celestial" displays, since they explode high in the night sky. What makes this particular celebration different from all the others is its *raison d'être.* Little by little the reader perceives that the occasion is not the Fourth of July (or a comparable Spanish holiday) but rather the Last Judgment. Postponed for thousands of years, to the despair of the faithful, the Day of Judgment has finally arrived. Surrounded by various saints and a flock of angels, God begins methodically blowing up the universe, star by star and planet by planet. Some of his heavenly companions are simply witnesses; others play a more active role. As the angels blast away with their twelve-gauge shotguns, Saint Mark sends a fiery bull to wreak death and destruction upon humanity. Like the Holy Church Fathers, the eleven thousand virgins martyred in Cologne by the Huns recoil in terror. Even Saint Vincent Ferrer and Saint Ignatius Loyola contribute to the chaos by setting off strings of firecrackers. The final *coup de grâce* is administered by Saint Barbara who, together with Pedro Botero (a folkloric figure identified with Satan), sets fire to a gigantic pile of fireworks. The resulting explosion not only extinguishes all human life but also blows the earth to smithereens. Contrary to T. S. Eliot's prediction in "The Hollow Men," the world ends with a bang rather than a whimper.

Eliodoro Puche

The second poem, by Eliodoro Puche, is short enough to quote in its entirety.

El camino nublado
asciende hasta la cima
del Sol.
        Mis pasos
y el aroma de mis primaveras muertas
        EL RELOJ
(fuga de las horas que caen)

c
o
m
o

l
a

p
l
o
m
a
d
a

TIENE EL DEDO EN LA BOCA

> [The cloudy path / leads to the Sun's / summit. / My steps / and the aroma of my dead primroses [or springs] / THE CLOCK / (flight of the hours that fall) / (like a plumb line) / HAS ITS FINGER IN ITS MOUTH]

Published in *Ultra* on May 21, 1921, "Silencio" recalls poems by Pierre Reverdy in which an earthly journey becomes a rite of passage during which the poet crosses from life into death. Like the French poet, Puche juxtaposes sparse, suggestive phrases to produce a drama of ellipsis. Like Reverdy, he creates an eerie silence in which the poem seems to exist outside time. Among other things, this suggests an explanation for the last, enigmatic line. While the image of the thumb-sucking clock was probably cultivated for its shock value, it dovetails nicely with the poem's larger preoccupations. For that matter, imagining a timepiece with fingers is no more ridiculous than speaking of the "hands" of a clock (the same expression exists in Spanish). The poet has simply taken the dead metaphor and developed it to its logical conclusion. Furthermore, the fact that the clock has its finger (minute hand) in its mouth means that its hands are no longer revolving. In other words, time has stopped altogether. This accords with what we already know about the poet's destination: the realm of death, where time stands still. We are left with the visual analogy of the plumb line—itself a metaphor for the "falling" hours—suspended vertically in the air. At some point, the reader realizes that the poet is evoking a grandfather clock and that the vertical phrase is intended to represent its pendulum. This identification confirms our earlier interpretation of the finger in the clock's mouth. Judging from its vertical position, moreover, the pendulum is stationary—another indication that the clock has stopped running. Hanging absolutely motionless, the pendulum symbolizes the plight of the poet himself, for whom time has ceased to exist.

3
Hispano-American Poetry

THE FIRST HISPANIC AMERICAN TO EXPERIMENT WITH VISUAL POETRY was the Chilean poet Vicente Huidobro, who published four examples in 1913.[1] Despite their undeniable historical importance, his initial attempts seem relatively unimaginative today. Inspired by traditional models dating back to the ancient Greeks, they were composed entirely of solid forms. Each text consisted of a series of horizontal verses whose length was varied to produce different pictorial contours. While three of the poems assumed abstract geometrical shapes, the fourth portrayed a recognizable object. In contrast to the former works, which evoked various Japanese themes, the latter depicted a village chapel crowned by a large cross. The second Hispanic American to explore the possibilities of visual poetry was the Mexican poet José Juan Tablada, beginning in 1915.[2] Entitled "Madrigales ideográficos," his first experiment combined two visual poems to form a single composition. Using outlined forms to portray a dagger and a high-heeled shoe, he created a dramatic still life. This work and a number of others were published in *Li-Po y otros poemas* in 1920. Unlike Huidobro's poems, which seem to have attracted little notice, Tablada's works received considerable publicity. Subsequent visual poets alternated between these two poles, between literary and artistic approaches. Some writers used words to create solid images, while others used them to depict an object's outline.

MEXICO

LUIS QUINTANILLA

For some reason, visual poetry never enjoyed the success in Hispanic America that it did in Europe, where it was extremely popular. Nevertheless, several poets in Mexico and Argentina experimented with the genre following the First World War. Since both countries harbored a flourishing avant-garde, this is not terribly surprising. Despite their relative isolation, artists and writers were well informed about the latest developments in Paris and Madrid. Encouraged by this supportive environment, a few individuals decided to try their hand at visual poetry. During the 1920s two competing factions existed in Mexico: the Contemporáneos, who had no official leader, and the Estridentistas ("Stridentists"), headed by Manuel Maples Arce. Embracing the period 1921–27, the second group was the more radical of the two and included poets, novelists, and artists. Luis Quintanilla, who liked to sign his last name Kin-Taniya, was one of the more interesting poets. A career diplomat like so many of his colleagues, he eventually acquired a PhD from Johns Hopkins and taught political science at several prominent universities. Aside from his academic credentials, what made him unique was the fact that he was born and raised in France. After visiting Mexico in 1917, however, he decided to renounce his French citizenship.

In 1923, Quintanilla published a slim book of poetry entitled *Avión* (*Airplane*). Not surprisingly, since his formative years were spent in Paris, the poems were written in the literary cubist mode. Utilizing discontinuity, dislocation, and displacement, they sought to reproduce modern reality. Although pictorial effects are few and far between, three of the compositions employ visual analogies. In a poem entitled "Hamaca," for example, a number of words are arranged in a semicircle to represent a hammock.[3] In "La pulga," by contrast, words are scattered about the page as if a pesky flea had invaded the poem. Entitled "Lluvia" ("Rain"), a third work strings words together like clothes drying on a line. Composed in October 1917, while Quintanilla was visiting Mexico, it combines water and music in equal proportions.

Gorgoritas que estallan
                    en el mojado asfalto
Resbaló un caballo
                    Abramos
La lluvia toca a mi ventana
Hay lágrimas de nube en la punta de cada hoja
y gotitas de leche en la punta de tus uñas sonrosadas

L	C	S	S	S
Á	O	O	I	O
G	N	B	E	B
R	H	R	N	R
I	A	E	T	E
M	S	L	O	M
A	T	A	C	I
S	Í	S	O	C
E	O	V	R	O
N	R	I	R	R
T	E	D	E	A
U	S	R	R	Z
C	B	I	L	Ó
A	A	E	A	N
R	L	R	L	M
A	A	A	L	O
	E	S	U	J
	L	G	V	A
	A	R	I	D
	G	I	A	O
	U	S		
	A	E		
		S		

S h t !
    es
        cu
            chad
e l s i le n c i o
Tu cabeza de niño
La frescura de tus labios
y tus ojos grises perdidos en el cabello
Resbala el agua en los pentagramas de líneas telefónicas
Formando notas incoloras sobre los alambres negros
        A veces caen
y tu dedo queda prendido
        a la tecla
Ya no se si es tu voz o el cantar de las nubes

[Musical notes that splash
on the wet asphalt
A horse slipped
Open up
The rain is knocking on my window
There are cloud tears on every leaf tip
and milky drops on the tips of your rosy nails

T	W	D	I	O
E	A	O	F	N
A	T	W	E	M
R	E	N	E	Y
S	R	T	L	H
O	W	H	T	U
N	E	E	H	M
Y	A	G	E	I
O	R	R	R	D
U	I	A	A	H
R	L	Y	I	E
F	Y	W	N	A
A	T	I	F	R
C	R	N	A	T
E	I	D	L	
	C	O	L	
	K	W	I	
	L	P	N	
	E	A	G	
	S	N		
		E		
		S		

Shh!
lis
ten
to
the silence
Your boyish head
The coolness of your lips
and your gray eyes lost in your hair
Water trickles down the telephone wires' stave
Forming colorless notes on the black wires
Sometimes they fall
and your finger lingers
on the piano key
I don't know if it is your voice or the clouds singing]

Although "Lluvia" is divided into three sections, these are linked together by their common imagery, thematics, and subject matter. The first stanza compares the raindrops to musical notes, the sound of tapping, and tears. The second establishes a parallel between the raindrops trickling down the window and tears running down the young woman's face. The third revives the comparison between the raindrops and music, and celebrates the woman's beauty. In contrast to the beginning and end, whose appearance is unremarkable, the middle section is more experimental. While any of the literary cubists could have written the rest of the poem, the central stanza was inspired by Guillaume Apollinaire. Like "Il pleut" ("It's Raining"), published in *SIC* the previous year, the second stanza is divided into five vertical lines that descend the page letter by letter.[4] Structured around identical metaphors, both poems establish a reciprocal relationship between rain and human tears. Whereas "Il pleut" evokes a series of bittersweet memories, "Lluvia" is primarily a love poem. Apollinaire is reminded of women's voices from the past, while Quintanilla marvels at his sweetheart's voice, which mingles with the gentle rain. Although it is difficult to be sure, she seems to be singing and accompanying herself on a piano. Thus the themes of rain, music, and voice finally merge in the last stanza. Recalling Shakespeare's "bare ruin'd choirs," the image of a musical stave composed of telephone wires is particularly effective. Inevitably, one wonders why the young woman is crying. Perhaps it is a sympathetic response to the rain, as in much of Verlaine's poetry. Or perhaps she is singing a sad song.

Salvador Novo

Although the journal from which the Contemporáneos group took its name was not founded until 1928, the movement itself began to coalesce about the same time as Estridentismo. Whereas the second school adopted a self-conscious avant-garde posture, the first embraced modern aesthetics with less fanfare but equal fervor. While the members collaborated on various projects and shared similar values, they felt no need to issue manifestos or other official proclamations. Equally at home in poetry or prose, Salvador Novo published no fewer than eight volumes in a single decade. For our purposes, the most interesting documents date from the beginning of his career. Between 1918 and 1923, he composed three visual poems entitled "Jarrón," "Mariposa," and "Buda."[5] Composed of solid forms, they depict a vase, a butterfly, and a statue of the Buddha.

The first poem was published initially in an avant-garde journal in Barcelona in 1922.[6] Except for the eight-point capitals in the first line, it could easily have been composed on a typewriter. The visual composition itself depicts a pot-bellied vase with a broad, flat lip. Indeed, the lip is as wide as the base. Nevertheless, since the vessel is tall and well-proportioned, it manages to look fairly graceful. Among other things, one wonders whether it is glass or ceramic.

LEVE JARRÓN
de tu
bello
vientre
surge dulce
olvidado son
marino, y entre
tu esbeltez
de viejas
rosas
hay
una
hez,
bello,
v i e j o,
e s b e l t o,
d u l c e j a r r ó n.

[HUMBLE VASE: a sweet, / forgotten sea / sound springs / from your / lovely / belly, / and dregs / remain / among / the slenderness / of old / roses, / lovely, / old, / slender, / sweet vase]

A modest little poem like its companions, "Jarrón" depicts a common household article that tends to be taken for granted. Thrust into the limelight, it is suddenly transformed from a simple utilitarian item into an object of admiration. As the poet examines the graceful vessel, turning it first one way and then the other, it awakens fond memories in him. Holding it up to his ear like a seashell, he listens to the sound of the sea emerging from its hollow depths. One wonders if this is merely an amusing whim or if the vase is somehow connected to the sea. Perhaps it comes from a Mediterranean country like Spain or Greece. Or perhaps it is a souvenir from the Gulf of Mexico. Leaning over to inspect the vase more closely, Novo catches a faint whiff of bygone roses. Again, one wonders if these are generic roses or if they are associated with a particular occasion. Who received the flowers in the first place? Who brought them to the house, and why? For better or worse, we never discover the answers to these questions. If the rosy residue provokes a Proustian experience, the poet prefers to contemplate it in private. Unlike Proust himself, who described his memories in loving detail, Novo only hints at the vase's fascinating history.

The second poem depicts a large yellow butterfly (possibly a Giant Sulphur) whose wings are fully extended. Between the creature's wings, one perceives its long, black body represented by the word "**MARIPOSA**" in boldface capitals. Although the antennae are invisible, Novo made the first letter larger than the others to represent its head. While that much is clear immediately, the visual perspective is rather ambiguous. Does the butterfly occupy a vertical position, like the vase in the previous poem, or does it occupy a horizontal position? Without additional information it is impossible to say. The creature could conceivably be sunning itself, or it could be a dead specimen pinned to the wall. Given the fact that visual poetry combines poetry and painting, this confusion is unavoidable. Since paintings are normally hung on the wall, viewers are accustomed to vertical portraits. Any other angle strikes them as unnatural. By contrast, since books are normally placed on a table, readers are used to horizontal texts. Our different motor habits reflect the physical demands imposed on us by different media.

Fortunately, as commonly happens in visual poetry, the text serves as a verbal corrective. As soon as we begin to decipher the poem, we discover that it depicts the butterfly from above. The text itself is divided into two columns separated by the word "**MARIPOSA**," which catches the reader's eye immediately. He or she is free accordingly to begin with this word or, as in the translation below, to leave it for later.

Vas		Vas
por los		por los
jardines de	**M**	jardines de
oro pimente	**A**	cacias y de
y eres paz	**R**	ubia arena.
en pos de	**I**	tus alas,
la dulce	**P**	étalos y
fuente.	**O**	nix son.
I leve	**S**	igue y
llueve	**A**	ma con
todo		todo
oro		oro

> [You pass / through / gardens of / golden peppers / as you peacefully / search for / the sweet / fountain. And all / the gold / lightly / rains down / **MARIPOSA** / You pass / through / gardens of / **A**cacias and / **B**londe sand. / **AND** your wings / are **P**etals and / **O**nyx. / **C**ontinue / along and / **L**ove with / all / the gold]

Since the visual design is remarkable for its symmetry, Novo decided to impose the same principle on the text as well. A rapid survey discloses symmetrical devices operating at the syntactical, lexical, and phonetic levels. Not only do the two columns utilize the same sentence structure initially, but they begin and end with the same words. Unlike the previous poem, which only flirted with the idea, "Mariposa" also introduces a complex rhyme scheme. In the first column, "vas" rhymes with "paz," "pimente" with "fuente," and "leve" with "llueve," in addition to numerous half rhymes. However, the second column is much less ambitious: only "son" rhymes with "con." Novo evidently grew tired of looking for words with the right length and the right sound. As generations of writers discovered before him, this is one of the disadvantages of using solid forms. All too frequently the poet is forced to adopt desperate measures. Novo omits definite and indefinite articles, for example, which are necessary to preserve the poetry's flow. Unable to find a rhyme for "fuente," he borrowed the word "pimiento" and transformed it into "pimente," a made-up word.

The fact that Novo speaks directly to the butterfly establishes a certain intimacy from the very beginning. He is obviously familiar with the creature and welcomes it to his garden. While the butterfly helps to pollinate the plants, its contribution is largely aesthetic. Watching it gliding this way and that, Novo marvels at its exceptional grace and beauty. As the butterfly seeks out nectar, it blends almost completely with its surroundings. Indeed, as the poet declares, it resembles a flower itself. The dominant color scheme is yellow—or, more precisely, yellow on yellow. The yellow butterfly is superimposed on a garden full of golden peppers, blossoming acacia trees, and blonde sand. As the sun rises higher in the sky, it seems to be raining gold. Among other things, the butterfly is associated with peace and love in Novo's mind. Since it represents a good omen, he wishes it well as it continues on its way.

Portraying a statue of the Buddha, the third poem is less successful than the first two compositions.

¡Oh!
Buda
de ruda
mirada de
bestia sa
grada, de
mística fe
e incienso de té.
Tú miras sin ver
las en todos los ma
res de micas, las per
las indemnes que en
modos solemnes indicas
para tus coll
ares. Y es dulce que el
cielo de un velo de tul
se despeje y deje al sol
tu testa enhiesta de un
gran caracol dorar. Se
esfuma la bruma . . . y es de
espuma el sol japonés. ¡Oh
Buda de cruda mirada . . . !

[Oh: / Buddha / with the dull / gaze of a / sacred beast, of / mystical faith / and wreathed in incense. / You look, without seeing / them in the mica / seas, at the peerless / pearls that in solemn ways / you indicate / for your necklaces. / How nice that the / sky veiled in tulle / has cleared up and has left / your great snail head / to turn brown in the sun. The / mist fades away . . . and the / Japanese sun is made of spray. / Oh! Buddha with the dull gaze . . . !]

This curious little poem may have been inspired by a visit to Japan or simply to a local art museum. At first glance, it strikes the reader as extraordinarily playful. Beginning with three sets of couplets, the rhymes come fast and furious with no perceptible pattern. In addition to a dozen rhymes, it possesses a lively rhythm and a lighthearted demeanor. Upon closer examination, however, the poem turns out to be extraordinarily undisciplined—it is not playful so much as lazy. Most of the rhymes have no other purpose than to amuse the reader. And not only has rhyming has become an end in itself, but there are far too many rhymes. Their density impedes the poem's flow and continually distracts the reader. Since end rhymes require a lot more effort, Novo constantly resorts to internal rhymes. For similar reasons, the poem consists almost entirely of run-on lines. Instead of ending a phrase when he reaches the edge of the visual image, Novo wraps it around and keeps on going. On five occasions, he simply slices a word in half as if it were a tomato or an onion.

Unfortunately, the visual image is no more rewarding than the text. Arranged to form a crude triangular shape, it looks more like a Christmas tree than a statue of a human being. Since there are so few visual cues, it is impossible to tell whether the figure is sitting or standing. On the one hand, the brief phrase "para tus coll" could depict the Buddha's feet, in which case he would be standing on a pedestal. On the other hand, the phrase could represent his hands joined together, in which case the following lines would represent the lower half of his body. Since the statue is exposed to the sun, we know it is located somewhere outdoors, either in a public park or in a private garden. It may be large and famous, like the statue at Kamakura, or it may be small and insignificant, perhaps a simple statuette. One thing is clear: this is not the jolly, pot-bellied figure so often seen in Chinese restaurants. Judging from the description, the statue depicts the Buddha clasping his prayer beads in one hand while engaged in meditation—one of several traditional poses. However, perhaps because he was a Roman Catholic, Novo seems to have had little sympathy for Eastern religions. Seeking to create a humorous portrait, he compares the Buddha to two animals: a (sacred) cow and a snail. The first image was inspired by the figure's impassive gaze, which struck Novo as essentially bovine. Like the veneration of cows in India, he implies, Buddhism is superstitious nonsense. The second comparison is equally uncomplimentary. Although statues of the ancient sage often show him wearing a bead cap, the present statue is bareheaded. Inspired by the Buddha's smooth dome, Novo depicts him as a slimy mollusk broiling in the sun. While his contemporaries may have found this portrait amusing, current readers can only shake their heads in wonder.

José María González de Mendoza

Of the various individuals who were aligned neither with the Estridentistas nor the Contemporáneos, the most important was undoubtedly José María González de Mendoza. Born in Spain, González was a prolific author who wrote under the pseudonym "El Abate de Mendoza" ("Father Mendoza") and who did much to advance the avant-garde cause in Mexico. Unfortunately, only a fraction of his writings has been collected to date. Beginning in 1923, he resided in Paris, where he studied at the Sorbonne, the Collège de France, and the École du Louvre. Like so many of his colleagues, he eventually entered the Mexican diplomatic corps and was attached to the legation in Paris. Some of his compositions appeared in reviews affiliated with the Contemporaries; others were published in journals associated with the Stridentists. At least one of his works was included in *Irradiador*, founded in 1923 by Manuel Maples Arce and Fermín Revueltas, which ceased publication a few months later. Whether González contributed to more than one issue is impossible to say, since no copies of the journal remain.

In 1927, a visual poem from *Irradiador* appeared in an article on Mexican poetry published in Argentina. Not only was it "a beautiful calligram," the author declared, but "perhaps the best poem the admirers of Maples Arce have produced."[7] Entitled "LA MARIMBA EN EL PATIO," it portrayed a joyful celebration.

E C S T A T I C M I N U E T
neighborhood
patio
O F T H E H O U S E S
S U N

children shouting
dogs barking BARKING
children shouting SHOUTS children
dogs barking BARKING dogs
children shouting

PANTINGSLAVEOF

B f p p f GU MOTORSAND OC
o l i e l I L CA
u a r n u LO owooooo SI
r g a n t TI ON a cat is sleeping
b s t a t NE ouuurrrruuuu AL
o e n e GA HO
n t r TE WL in the shade
s i
n
g

at 40 an hour
time is sweating minutes

Depicting a festive gathering, this charming little poem is surprisingly sophisticated and yet surprisingly simple. Although some of the elements have little or no pictorial value, it contains at least five visual analogies. With a little effort, the reader/viewer can detect the sun's circular outline, the patio gate's rectangular frame, and the marimba itself at the bottom of the page. González enlarges the central letter in "SOL," traces the gate's outline, and makes each letter in "MARIMBA" larger than the preceding one. This device resembles the very first visual analogy, invented in January 1914 by Francesco Cangiullo, who subjected the word FUMARE ("TO SMOKE") to the same procedure.[8] The marimba itself suffers from the same ambiguous perspective as Salvador Novo's butterfly, discussed previously. In contrast to the other objects in the picture, which are viewed from the side, it is portrayed from above. Viewed from the perspective (and the position) of the musician, the seven letters represent the instrument's rosewood keyboard. While the marimba player himself is not visible, we learn he is being paid forty pesos an hour.

Directly above the instrument, one notes six parallel diagonal lines that seem to represent falling rain. Like Luis Quintanilla before him, González borrowed this device from Apollinaire's poem "Il pleut," where it serves a similar purpose.[9] Although the festivities could conceivably be interrupted by a sudden shower, the adjective "alegre" ("lively") suggests the rain is purely metaphorical. The poet is merely comparing the marimba's cascading notes to raindrops. This impression is reinforced by the presence of the verb "tocar," which means "to play (a musical instrument)." Unfortunately, we never learn the reason for the animated

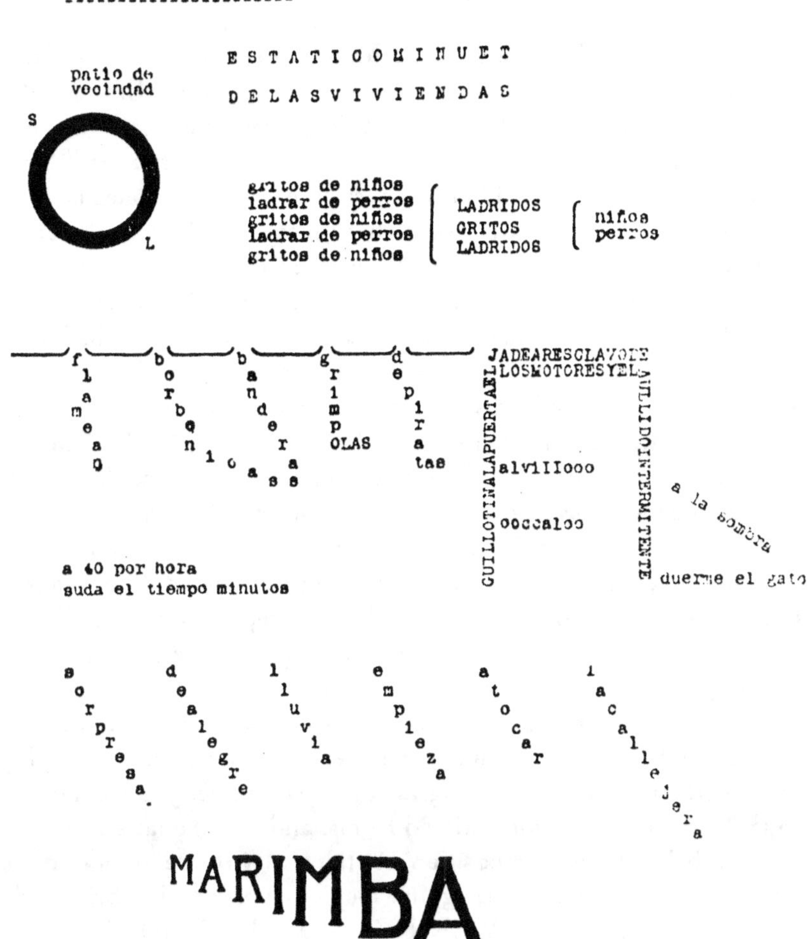

7. José María González de Mendoza, "LA MARIMBA EN EL PATIO"

gathering. If the Bourbon flag hints at a political agenda, the pirate flags suggest another, completely different interpretation. The occasion could be a national holiday, or then again it could simply be a child's birthday. Whatever the explanation, everyone is obviously having a good time. Competing with noisy children and barking dogs, the marimba's music fills the whole neighborhood until the houses themselves seem to dance. Completely oblivious to the joyful celebration, a little cat snoozes quietly in the shade.

José D. Frías

During 1923 and 1924, González de Mendoza spent much of his time with another Mexican expatriate, the poet José D. Frías, who served as foreign correspondent for *El Universal.* Among other things, they amused themselves by sending humorous compositions to various friends.[10] Since the two men subscribed to different literary theories, González later recalled, their collaboration was somewhat uneven. "Frías's work can be classified as Symbolist," he explained, "whereas my preference is for the poetry that Guillaume Apollinaire associated with 'l'esprit nouveau,' which others have nicknamed 'cubist,' and for haiku poetry, which José Juan Tablada introduced into Spanish." The prototype for their collaborative ventures, he added, was a congratulatory poem sent to the writer Francisco Orozco Muñoz on his saint's day (October 4, 1923). Although much of the composition was written in traditional verse, it concluded with four visual poems. Three of the texts were authored by Frías and translated into visual terms by González, who created the last poem himself.

The fact that the compositions are handwritten adds to their considerable charm. The problem with mechanical reproduction, as Walter Benjamin pointed out, is that it destroys the original work's "aura."[11] Unlike poetry in print, which looks cold and unresponsive, the four poems possess an undeniable presence. Not only are they more expressive, but they also create a certain intimacy between poet and reader. That they are modeled on Apollinaire's calligrams and haiku poetry is plain to see. Like the former, they favor outlined forms, and like the latter, they are extremely brief. Each composition contains a witty reference to the fact that Orozco is living in Belgium. Depicting an arching bridge, the first poem proclaims: "BETWEEN MY POVERTY AND BRUGES THERE IS ALAS NO BRIDGE." Known as the "Venice of the North," Bruges is famous for its beautiful canals and its countless bridges. Unfortunately, the authors joke, none of them stretch as far as Paris. On another level, to be sure, the poem seems to have served as an apology. Although Orozco had doubtless invited his two friends to visit him in Belgium, they complain they can't afford the trip.

The second text portrays another object traditionally associated with Belgium: a mug of beer (apparently resting on a table). "LET'S HAVE A BEER," it reads; "THE SUN HAS ALREADY SET IN FLANDERS." This is an updated version of an old joke: since it is always dark somewhere in the world, it is always time to start drinking. Imbibers who live in Belgium have an advantage over their counterparts in Paris be-

8. José D. Frías, Visual Poems

cause, although they share the same time zone, it gets dark there earlier. The third work was suggested by an idiomatic expression involving Belgium: "CUANDO CLAVARÉ MI PICA EN FLANDES" ("WHEN I WILL ACCOMPLISH WONDERS"). The humor here derives from the clash between its actual sense and its literal sense: "WHEN I WILL PLANT MY PIKE IN FLANDERS." Focusing on the second meaning, the visual image portrays a medieval lance. Conceived as a "caligrama cardíaco," the fourth poem assumes a solid form. Authored by González alone, the heart-shaped composition reads: "MY HEART HAS TRANSFORMED ITSELF INTO A FOUNTAIN PEN MY FRIEND." Structured around a pair of metonyms, this statement operates on two different levels. On the one hand, it is meant to be amusing—the image of a heart morphing into a fountain pen is worthy of the Surrealists. On the other hand, it has a serious purpose as well. Since González cannot visit his friend in Belgium, he promises to write to him instead.

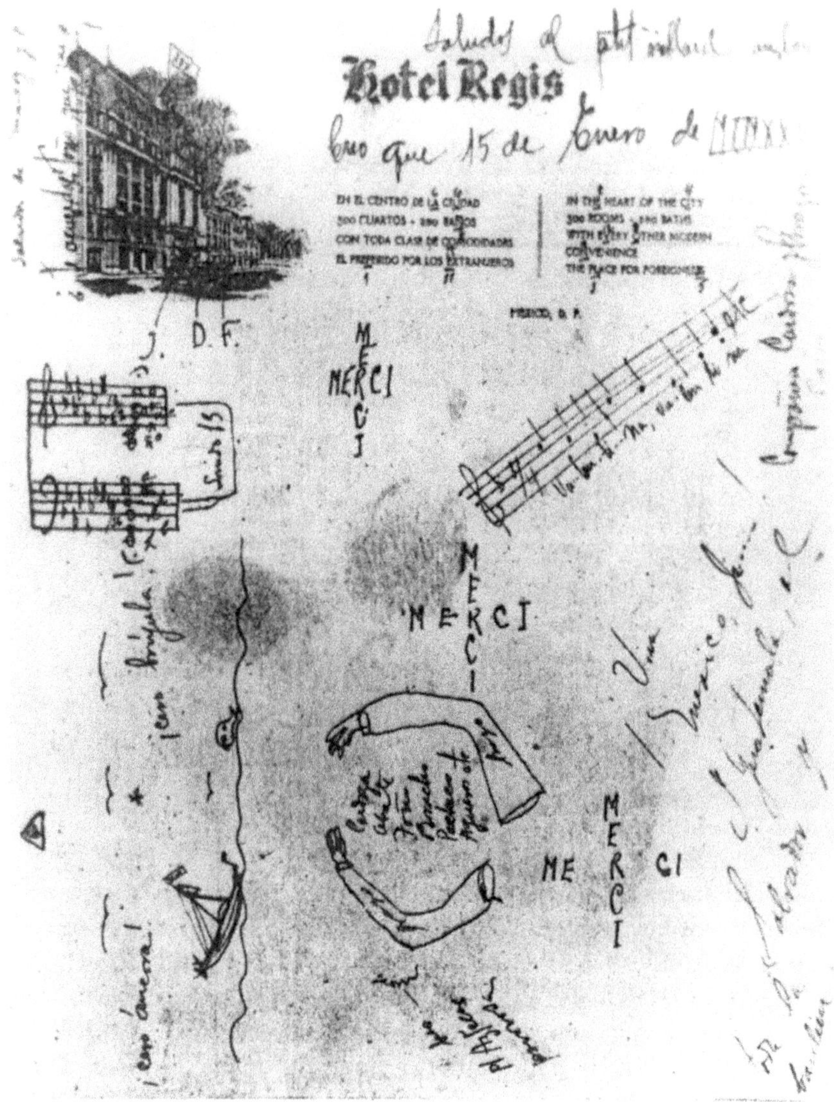

9. José D. Frías and José María González de Mendoza, "Feliz Año Nuevo"

After Frías returned to Mexico in October 1924, leaving González in Paris, the two men began to exchange humorous letters. On January 15, 1925, Frías sent his friend a curious calligrammatic composition. Written on the stationary of the Hotel Regis, where he was staying, it juxtaposes random thoughts and impressions to form a verbo-visual collage. At the top, Frías numbers various letters of the hotel's letterhead in such a way that they spell "Feliz Año Nuevo" ("Happy New Year"). Accompanied by snatches of music, one of which is addressed to "Valentina," a cruciform refrain extends from upper left to lower right, expressing his repeated "MERCI" ("THANKS"). Toward the bottom, two disembodied arms embrace a list of the poet's friends in Paris, whom he obviously missed. These include González himself, the Guatemalan poet Luis Cardoza y Aragón, and four other individuals. Besides additional greetings scribbled to Cardoza and a "petit milord anglais" ("little English lord"), the margins contain a celebration of Latin American solidarity involving Mexico, Guatemala, El Salvador, and "toda la banlieu" ("the whole neighborhood.") At the bottom of the page, Frías placed a tiny caricature of himself, seen in profile, uttering the words "beso p[ara] / Azteca pavorosa" ("a kiss f[or] / the terrifying Aztec." According to González, the "Azteca" was a female acquaintance from Mexico who never stopped talking.

ARGENTINA

Alberto Hidalgo

Alberto Hidalgo was a prolific poet who served as a conduit between Europe and Latin America. Born in Peru, he settled in Buenos Aires in 1920 and played an important role in the local avant-garde. Although his first few volumes of poetry were published in Peru, the remainder of his work appeared in Argentina, where he spent the rest of his life. While Hidalgo was attracted to Italian Futurism, he was well acquainted with modern French poetry and with literary events taking place in Spain. Since he lived for a while in both Paris and Madrid, he got to know the various schools of poetry at first hand.[12] In 1923, he published a book of avant-garde poetry that synthesized the most recent developments in Europe. Entitled *Química del espíritu* (*Chemistry of the Spirit*), it combined assorted sound effects and visual notations in a highly original way.[13] Among other things, six visual poems were sprinkled throughout the volume.

Although we know Hidalgo was familiar with Apollinaire's poetry, only one of the compositions recalls *Calligrammes*. Entitled "Sabiduría" ("Wisdom"), it bears a superficial resemblance to "Il pleut."[14] In both works, several parallel lines of poetry descend the page letter by letter like raindrops. Whereas Apollinaire's poem reads from top to bottom, however, Hidalgo's text flows in the opposite direction. While "Il pleut" depicts rain streaming down a window pane, the parallel lines in "Sabiduría" represent music, smoke, and the poet's soul.

		a		y
		d		
		a		é
		ll	O	l
o		o	M	
m	a	h	U	m
u	d	n	S	e
h	a	i		
	r		U	d
n	i	a	T	i
u	m	d	I	ó
		n	R	
o	i	e	Í	p
m	m	s	P	o
o			S	r
c	ó	a	E	
	g	n		c
a	l	u	l	o
í	o		a	n
b	c	e		s
u		d	s	e
s	e		e	j
	s	a	r	o
a		d	i	
c	o	n	a	q
i	m	e		u
s	u	s	s	e
ú	h		o	
m		a	l	n
	e	l		o
a	s		n	
l	e	e	e	c
		d		r
e	e		é	e
d	d	a	r	y
		c	t	e
l	a	s	n	r
a	l	u	o	a
r	o	b	c	
i	c		n	e
p		n	e	n
s	a	e		
e	l		o	n
		í	l	a
a	e	u	ó	d
l	d	f	s	a

[the spiraling music ascended like smoke
my gaze fastened on the last wisp of smoke
I searched for the trail of an untraveled path
but only encountered the SUPREME SPIRIT
who advised me not to believe in anything]

From the beginning, Hidalgo was faced with a conflict between literary and artistic conventions. If the text began at the top and descended the page, the verbal flow would contradict the visual flow, which, dominated by images of music and smoke, was clearly upward. If the text began at the bottom and ascended the page, the verbal flow would coincide with the visual flow, but would violate normal reading procedure. Hidalgo chose the second solution as the lesser of the two evils. Since the first four vertical lines extend from earth to heaven, they flow in that direction. However, since the fifth line extends from heaven to earth, it flows in the opposite direction. Despite its visual pyrotechnics, "Sabiduría" turns out to be surprisingly traditional. The text consists of five lines rhyming ABBAB with five beats to each line. As such it combines the calligram with one of Spain's oldest and most illustrious verse forms: the *copla de arte mayor*. The latter choice lends a dignified air to the poem, which recounts Hidalgo's quest for wisdom. While the first four lines chronicle his search for truth, the fifth records his inevitable disappointment. According to the Supreme Being himself, truth is as evanescent as music or smoke. Like everything else in the world, it is simply an illusion. Hidalgo finally acquires the wisdom he has been seeking, but it is fraught with cynical uncertainty.

In contrast to "Sabiduría," which was inspired by a French poem, the remaining works recall several atypical Ultraist experiments. Whereas the first composition depicts a recognizable scene, the others tend to be largely abstract. At most they employ an occasional visual analogy. Embodying a minimalist aesthetic, "Suicidio" and its companions resemble sketches rather than formal paintings.

❋

a
n
u

a

é
r
i

e
m

z
u
l

e
d

o
l
i
h

n
u

r
o
p

suicidio

al norte
al sur,
al este,
al oeste,
siempre la cara de la vulgaridad.
mas, un día
con pasaporte de smith wesson,

[to the north / to the south, / to the east, / to the west, / always the face of vulgarity. / but one day, / with a smith and wesson passport, / I will ride a beam of light to a ❋]

Like the first four verses of "Sabiduría," the final line reverses the normal reading order. Although the visual line extends from the star to Hidalgo, he plans to ride it upward to its source. Instead of writing the word "estrella," Hidalgo replaces it with a picture of a star. On another level, of course, the line represents the poet's soul ascending toward heaven.

Although suicide is not usually something to joke about, the poem expresses a common and very human sentiment. Bombarded by vulgarity from every direction, we occasionally feel like taking a pistol and blowing our brains out. Frantz Fanon speaks for us all when he remarks: "There are too many imbeciles on earth."[15] Rather than a threat to commit suicide, therefore, the poem is an expression of frustration. It basically acts as a safety valve, allowing Hidalgo to vent his annoyance.

Entitled "Choque de trenes" ("Colliding trains"), the third composition evokes another unfortunate aspect of modern life. Like the previous poem, it represents an exercise in minimalist poetics.

el ruido de la ruda colisión.
a lo lejos el viento repetía

pron pron pron pron pron pron
pron pron pron pron pron pron

marchaban ambos por la misma vía, nózaroc le otnup la ovuted sel es

[the noise of the terrible collision.
in the distance the wind repeated
pron pron pron pron pron pron
pron pron pron pron pron pron
both were moving along the same track, tniop emas eht ta deppots straeh rieht.]

In only four or five lines, "Choque de trenes" manages to violate every reading convention imaginable. Ironically, despite its chaotic appearance, the poem is carefully organized. The problem with the minimalist aesthetic is that it doesn't leave poets (or artists) much to work with. Reviewing his limited resources, Hidalgo devised an ingenious plan. The last line would contain two sentences that would collide—like the trains in the title. In order to accomplish this, the second sentence would need to be printed backwards. The last line would also serve as the first line. Hoping to quell the confusion, Hidalgo added a set of instructions. Readers should proceed from bottom to top, he explained, and should read the second verse from right to left. Although the poem could have been structured from the top down, this allowed him to depict the sounds of the collision rising into the air. Despite its radical appearance, the text turns out to be surprisingly regular. At first glance, it appears to consist of four twelve-syllable lines rhyming ABAB. Sooner or later, however, one perceives that the twelve "prons" constitute a fifth line. Like "Sabiduría," the composition is composed of five verses rhyming ABBAB.

At some point, one hopes, the reader also realizes the poem is not about trains. Or rather, that the title is merely a metaphor. More precisely, since references to a train wreck occur elsewhere in the work, it represents an extended metaphor. In reality, the composition describes two individuals who suddenly fall in love. The first indication that it is concerned with human subjects (and with love) occurs in the second line, where the word "corazón" is introduced. The thought of two locomotives suffering heart attacks is ludicrous. In addition, the poem contains a number of words that are deliberately ambiguous. Like "marchar," for example, which describes many kinds of locomotion, "vía" designates many different paths. Similarly, "al punto" can be translated as "immediately" or "suddenly." With a little effort, one can reconstruct the encounter described in the poem. The man and the woman were walking along obliviously when they suddenly glimpsed each other. Or they may have actually bumped into each other. In either case, they fell head over heels in love. The French compare love at first sight to being hit by a bolt of lightning (*un coup de foudre*). Hidalgo compares it to a collision between two trains. The experience was so violent for both individuals that their hearts stopped for a moment. By the time they regained their composure, their hearts were beating so furiously ("pron, pron, pron") that they could be heard from a distance.

The next poem is considerably less ambitious and, perhaps as a result, less successful. Entitled "Elevación," it depicts an urban scene bathed in moonlight.

a
í
b
u
s

e
t
s
o
p

n
u

a
í
b
u
s

a
í
s
e
f
i
e
l
p

a
l
r
i
d
n
e
calle. dormita la ciudad con una r
r
o
p

inefable quietud. hacia la luna

> [street. the city is dozing with an / ineffable stillness. toward the moon / to render homage rising a pole was rising]

Like most of Hidalgo's visual poems, "Elevación" utilizes a traditional verse form, which it has modified according to its own specifications. Rhyming AABB, the text consists of two couplets of unequal length. The first two lines contain twelve syllables, the second two lines nine syllables. The insistence on using regular verse forms explains several puzzling features. The first line begins with the single word "calle," followed by a period, because Hidalgo needed two more syllables. "Subía" is repeated twice in the last line because the line was originally three syllables short. The tense changes from the present to the imperfect for no apparent reason so that the verb will rhyme with "pleitesía." Hidalgo displays the same fondness for vertical forms reading from bottom to top that we have encountered previously. Although the scene takes place in a city, the visual design consists of two horizontal lines and an upright. There is nothing that specifically evokes an urban setting. We could be virtually anywhere. Like the trees, the cars, and the buildings that presumably line the street, the moon overhead is completely invisible. All we see is a telephone pole rising into the air. Ironically, since "poste" has several meanings, we cannot even be sure of that. It may be a pillar of some sort, or even a pylon.

At first glance, the fifth poem appears to be completely abstract. Entitled "El destino," it is arranged to form a perfect circle composed of four irregular verses rhyming ABBA:

> en medio de la tierra, que es suspiro
> vagabundo de dios, el hombre es punto
> perdido. ¡es un asunto
> para pegarse un tiro!

> [in the middle of the earth, which is a sigh / god's vagabond: man is a tiny / dot. it is enough / to make you scream!]

As the poem proclaims, mankind's destiny is totally insignificant. Despite our inflated opinion of ourselves and our creations, we play a miniscule role in the universe. To be sure, this view conflicts with the traditional view of Christianity, which, like Judaism and Islam, is relentlessly homocentric. According to Christian dogma, God witnesses every one of our actions. Nothing escapes His attention. In reality, Hidalgo declares, nothing could be further from the truth. Viewed from

el destino

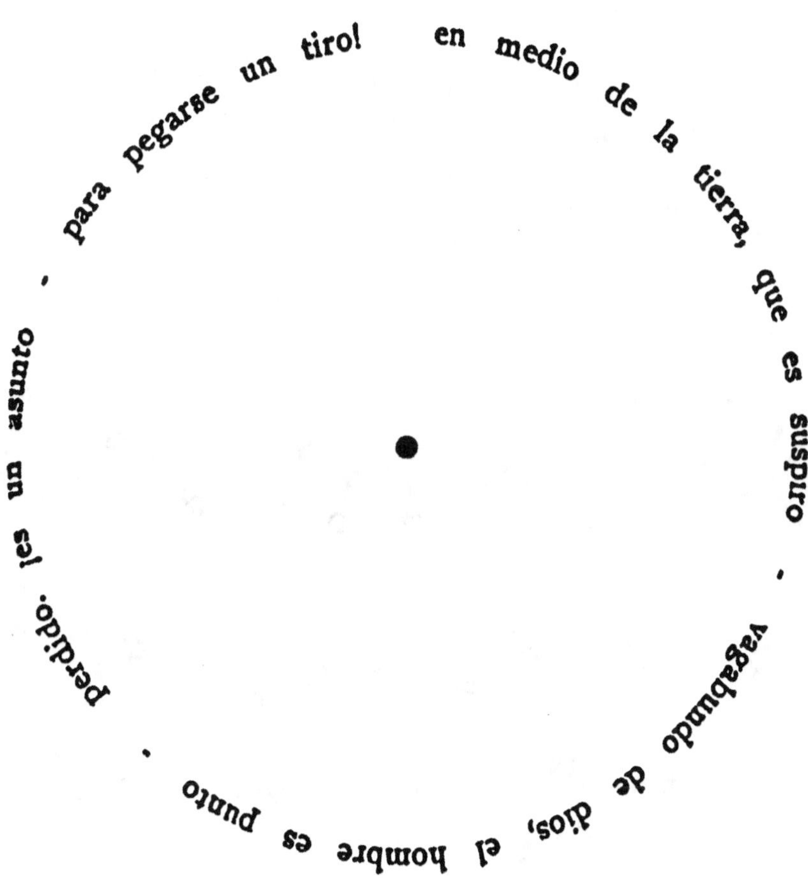

10. Alberto Hidalgo, "El destino"

God's perspective, man is no larger than an ant—and no more significant. This observation has important implications. God is not dead after all, as Nietzsche announced long ago; He is simply disinterested. Human beings matter very little in the grand scheme of things. Their self-important posturing is enough to make one scream. Complementing these observations, the visual design depicts three different objects simultaneously: the earth, an eye, and a target. Continuing the dominant metaphor, man is portrayed as an insignificant dot in (or on) the world. The eye in

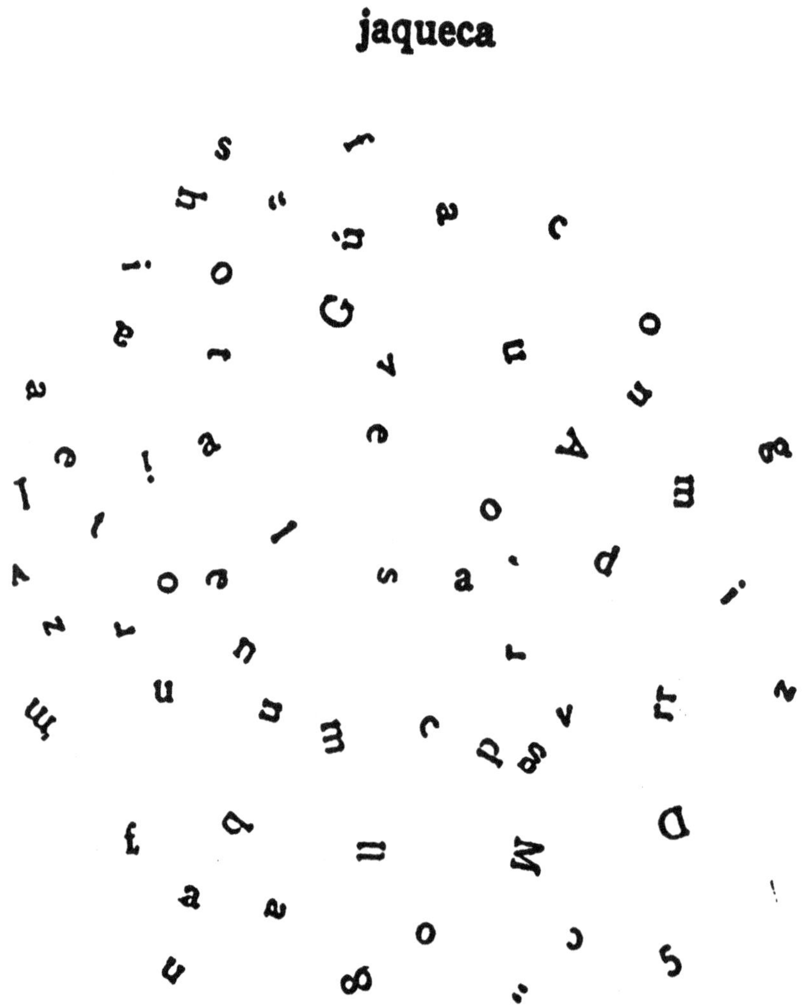

11. Alberto Hidalgo, "Jaqueca"

question belongs to God, who sees everything but regards humanity with indifference. The third image stems from a play on words. In addition to the translation given above, "pegarse un tiro" means "to fire a shot." In this case, the shot seems to be directed at mankind, which has become a target of ridicule.

Entitled "Jaqueca" ("Migraine"), the final composition is in some ways the most adventurous. Unlike some of the preceding works, which employ visual analogies, it is entirely abstract. The only clue to its identity is provided by the title, which provides remarkably little information. Whereas most of the previous poems contain rhyming phrases, "Jaqueca" contains no phrases at all. For that matter, it contains no words. Consisting of a ball of letters, numerals, and punctuation marks, it looks more like a tumbleweed than a poem. There seems to be no coherent principle underlying the text other than random distribution. However, the absence of logical coherence does not mean the work has ceased to signify. The typographical jumble represents the pain and confusion produced by migraine headaches. Since the letters have no independent life of their own, the distinction between picture and text ceases to exist. The verbal elements function exclusively as visual counters. While the composition possesses the superficial attributes of a poem, it acts exactly like a painting.

Oliverio Girondo

Thanks to an agreement whereby he promised to study law if his parents sent him abroad every year, Oliverio Girondo vacationed in Europe annually between 1905 and 1922. Most of his time was spent in Paris, where Jules Supervielle introduced him to avant-garde literature and where he witnessed several Dada manifestations. Using cubist techniques to achieve some of the Dadaist goals, his own poetry is humorous, fragmentary, and often outrageous. The collection of poems for which Girondo is best known is entitled *Veinte poemas para ser leídos en el tranvía* (*Twenty Poems to Be Read on the Streetcar*) (1922). Written largely in prose and accompanied by his own illustrations, they earned him a reputation as one of the most advanced poets in Argentina. During the next ten years, he published two volumes of poetry that confirmed his reputation as an *enfant terrible: Calcomanías* (*Decals*) (1925) and *Espantapájaros* (*Scarecrows*) (1932). Inspired by the second book's title, Girondo created a poem in the shape of a scarecrow, which he placed at the very beginning.

According to Thorpe Running, this composition marked "the height of his development as a vanguardist."[16]

Yo no sé nada
Tú no sabes nada
Ud. no sabe nada
Él no sabe nada
Ellos no saben nada
Ellas no saben nada
Uds. no saben nada
Nosotros no sabemos nada

La desorientación de mi generación tiene su explicación en la
dirección de nuestra educación, cuya idealización de la acción,
era—¡sin discusión – una mistificación, en contradicción con
nuestra propensión a la meditación, a la
contemplación y a la masturbación.

(Guteral, lo más guturalmente
que se pueda). Creo que creo
en lo que creo que no creo.
Y creo que no creo en
lo que creo que creo.

"Cantar de las ranas"

¡ Y ¡Y ¿A ¿A ¡Y ¡Y

su ba llí llá su ba
bo jo es es bo jo
las las tá? tá? las las
es es ¡A ¡A es es
ca ca quí cá ca ca
le le no no le le
ras ras es es ras ras
arri aba tá tá arri aba
ba! .. jo! .. ! .. ! .. ba! .. jo! ..[17]

Compared to most of the visual poems we have examined previously, Girondo's composition looks rather primitive. The scarecrow's head is square instead of circular, for example, and it seems to have six legs. Despite an attempt to soften its silhouette, the latter is relentlessly rectilinear—doubtless because the poem was composed on a typewriter. In short, the figure resembles a robot more than a scarecrow. While the head and body consist of solid forms, the legs (two as it turns out) are outlined. The original poem was considerably more colorful than the black and white version reproduced above. The arms and upper torso (lines 9–13) were printed in red, as were the belt (line 19) and the stripe running down each leg. Like the visual image, the text is divided into four sections: the head, the chest, the stomach, and the legs. Each of these is separated from the others by a horizontal space. As Running remarks, the poem illustrates Girondo's "deeply entrenched dadaist approach to life."[18] In addition, it questions several key presuppositions underlying traditional Western philosophy. The first section attacks the Cartesian foundations of knowledge:

> I don't know anything
> You [familiar singular] don't know anything
> You [formal singular] don't know anything
> He doesn't know anything
> They [masculine] don't know anything
> They [feminine] don't know anything
> You [formal plural] don't know anything
> We don't know anything.

Two things are worth noting about this imaginary grammatical exercise. In the first place, it represents a partial declension of the verb "saber." Girondo has omitted four conjugations: the third person feminine singular ("Ella"), the first person feminine plural ("Nosotras"), the second person masculine plural ("Vosotros"), and the second person feminine plural ("Vosotras"). The reasons for this choice seem to have been purely visual. Girondo wanted the head to be square rather than rectangular, and he did not want conjugations that would stick out the side. In the second place, the order in which the declension normally proceeds is reversed in the last four lines. The section ends not with a third person accusation but with a sobering admission: "Nosotros no sabemos nada." The declension has escalated from a simple grammatical exercise to a universal declaration. While we think we know something, in reality we know nothing at all. The recognition that knowledge is essentially illusory embraces all of humanity.

As Jorge Schwartz observes, the constant repetition of "nada" relentlessly hammers this point home.[19] Like a religious litany, it engenders a visceral as well as an intellectual response. A similar reiterative structure governs the next two sections, which attack rational thought:

> The disorientation of my generation derives its explanation from the direction of our education, whose idealization of action was—without further discussion—a mystification, in contradiction to our inclination to meditation, contemplation, and masturbation.
> (Guttural, as gutturally as possible). I believe
> I believe in that which I believe I do not believe. And I believe
> I do not believe in that which I believe I believe.

The second section introduces the theme of disorientation, which Girondo develops in the following section. Stringing nouns together that simply end in –ion, he parodies the latinate discourse of his former professors while managing to make a certain amount of sense. The confusion that bedevils his generation, Girondo declares, stems from the fact that the school system valued sports more than activities of the mind. The rest of the section parodies the Cartesian method and its faith in logical reasoning. Each of the two statements about believing—one positive, the other negative—contradicts itself. Each undermines its own authority, therefore, and demonstrates the fallibility of belief in general. Descartes falls into a similar trap, Girondo implies, when he announces "I think, therefore I am." What he is really saying is "I think, therefore I think I am." In the absence of any objective proof, his conclusion is simply based upon belief.

Since the poem is not a philosophical treatise but a Dada exercise, Girondo introduces a little humor at this point. Unexpectedly, a "Song of the Frogs" fills the air, alternating between high-pitched Y's and basso profundo A's. In reality, the creatures have been serenading the reader for some time. This is why Girondo insisted the "creos" and "no creos" be pronounced as gutturally as possible—so that they would sound like a chorus of frogs. The poem concludes with the narrator restlessly searching for something.

> And I go up the stairs! . .
> And I go down the stairs! . .
> Is it there? It isn't here! . .
> Is it there? It isn't here! . .
> And I go up the stairs! . .
> And I go down the stairs! . .

Unlike the rest of the text, which reads from left to right and from top to bottom, the final section reverses this procedure. Recalling Apollinaire's

"Il pleut" and Quintanilla's "Lluvia," six diagonal lines forming the scarecrow's legs descend the page syllable by syllable. On the one hand, to be sure, they depict the figure's striped trousers. With a little effort we can even make out a pair of shoes. On the other hand, they represent Girondo descending the staircase over and over. Unexpectedly, the reading sequence mimics the actions of the poet himself. Chronicling the latter's quest for certainty, this section concludes the attack on Cartesian rationalism with a striking metaphor. Searching for certainty in an uncertain universe, Girondo declares, is like endlessly running up and down a set of stairs. If what you are looking for is not there, you are never going to find it.

4

French Poetry after Apollinaire

BETWEEN 1914 AND 1918, WHEN HE DIED AT THE AGE OF ONLY 38, Guillaume Apollinaire created approximately 150 *calligrammes*. Following his impressive example, many poets experimented with visual poetry in France following and even during the First World War. Amédée Ozenfant, who would go on to found Purism with Le Corbusier, edited a journal entitled *L'Elan* from April 1915 to December 1, 1916. Since he was an artist, he was interested in enhancing the genre's visual aspect. During 1916 Ozenfant conducted a series of daring experiments that succeeded in transforming typography into an art form. In addition to the attractive layout he designed for the journal, some of the characters were hand painted. In February 1916, he explained that these were experiments in "PSYCHOTYPE, an art that consists in making the typographical characters participate in the expression of thought and the painting of various moods, NO LONGER AS CONVENTIONAL SIGNS BUT AS SIGNS HAVING SIGNIFICANCE IN THEMSELVES."[1]

TRISTAN TZARA

Typographical effects played a significant role in Dada poetry as well.[2] In 1919, for example, Tristan Tzara published a poem entitled "**BILAN**" ("**BALANCE-SHEET**") that employed twenty different typefaces.

arc voltaïque de ces deux nerfs qui ne se touchent pas

près du coeur

on constate le frisson noir sous une lentille

est-ce sentiment ce blanc jaillissement

et l'amour méthodique

partage en rayons mon corps

pâte dentifrice

billets

transatlantique

la foule casse la colonne couchée du vent

éventail de fusées

sur ma tête

la revanche sanglante du two-step libéré

RÉPERTOIRE DE PRÉTENTIONS À PRIX FIXE

folie à 3 heures 20

ou 3 Frs. 50

la cocaïne ronge pour son plaisir lentement les murs

horoscope satanique se dilate sous ta vigueur

VIGILANCE DE VIRGILE VÉRIFIE LE VENT VIRIL

des yeux tombent encore[3]

> [electric arc of these two nerves which are not touching / near the heart / one notes the black shudder beneath a lens / is this white spurt sentiment / and methodical love / parcels out my body in beams / toothpaste / tickets / oceanliner / the crowd fractures the wind's recumbent column / fan of signal flares / above my head / the bloody revenge of the liberated two-step / repertory of pretensions at a fixed price / madness at 3:20 / or 3 francs 50 centimes / cocaine derives pleasure from slowly gnawing the walls / satanic horoscope expands beneath your vigor / virgil's vigilance verifies the viril wind / eyes are still falling]

This transcription does not do justice to the original version, which features the title in huge letters at the upper left and the silhouette of a black hand pointing to the author's signature at the lower right. With one exception (a line printed in small capitals), the work is composed exclusively of lower case letters. Most of the typographical effects are fairly simple. Tzara varies the size of the fonts, their style, or both. Since the poem occupied an oversized page originally, the characters vary from eight to twenty-two points. Besides roman, italic, boldface, and cursive letters, it includes many other styles. Since the composition contains exactly twenty lines, each of which employs a different typeface, no two lines look exactly the same. "The variation in the letters and the typographical styles," Henri Béhar observes, "emphasizes the aggressiveness and the logical disorder of a poem with an amorous subtext."[4] Indeed, the poem fairly crackles with sexual electricity from beginning to end. The apparently nonsensical title establishes the basic paradigm. Like parallel debit and credit columns, Tzara and an anonymous woman are standing (or perhaps lying) side by side. The abundance of orgasmic imagery suggests that they soon find themselves making love.

As "**BILAN**" demonstrates, Dada poems came to resemble posters before long, and Dada posters came to resemble poems. Their experimental typography not only advertised their decisive break with the past but also made them instantly appealing. Like Tzara, André Breton and other future Surrealists also experimented with typographical effects. Indeed, the First Surrealist Manifesto (1924) devoted several pages to the genre.[5] Seeking ways to produce unexpected associations, Breton juxtaposed newspaper headlines to form a series of short "poems," such as "Un éclat de rire / de saphir dans l'île de Ceylan" ["A burst of sapphire / laughter on the island of Ceylon"] and "Un saut dans le vide / **UN**

CERF" ["A leap into the void / a deer."] If visual poetry can be defined as poetry that is meant to be seen, as I proposed earlier, "**BILAN**" and its companions certainly fit this definition. And yet, on closer examination the typographical exercises seem to be largely decorative. Despite their undeniable visual appeal, they contribute little or nothing to the poem's meaning. The verbal and visual elements fail to interact in a significant manner, or they do so to a minimal degree. The problem with Behar's analysis of "**BILAN**" is not that it is wrong but that it lacks specificity. Most Dada poems, regardless of their typography, display "aggressiveness and logical disorder."

André Breton

While André Breton is best known as the founder (or cofounder) of the Surrealist movement, his first attempts at writing poetry were far from revolutionary. Like most French poets at the beginning of the twentieth century, he chose to write in the Symbolist mode. However, other poets were experimenting with a new kind of poetry, one that reflected recent advances in communication and transportation. Breton was attracted to both schools and developed close ties to their respective leaders. A tug of war ensued between Paul Valéry, the leader of the Symbolists, and Guillaume Apollinaire, the leader of the avant-garde, who convinced Breton to join him and his friends.[6] Although Apollinaire succumbed to the Spanish flu a few years later, he was one of the key formative influences in the younger poet's life.[7] Inspired by *Calligrammes*, for instance, Breton briefly experimented with visual effects in his own poetry. Published in *Dada* in March 1920, one of the more captivating experiments was entitled "Pièce fausse."

Du vase en cristal de Bohême
Du vase en cris
Du vase en cris
Du vase en
En cristal
Du vase en cristal de Bohême
Bohême
Bohême
En cristal de Bohême
Bohême
Bohême
Bohême
Hême hême oui Bohême
Du vase en cristal de Bo Bo
Du vase en cristal de Bohême
Aux bulles qu'enfant tu soufflais
Tu soufflais
Tu soufflais
Flais
Flais
Tu soufflais
Qu'enfant tu soufflais
Du vase en cristal de Bohême
Aux bulles qu'enfant tu soufflais
Tu soufflais
Tu soufflais
Oui qu'enfant tu soufflais
C'est là c'est là tout le poème
Aube éphé
Aube éphé
Aube éphémère de reflets
Aube éphé
Aube éphé
Aube éphémère de reflets.[8]

The first thing one notices is that the vase evoked in the first line is depicted visually. Unfortunately, since the text is rarely printed on a single page, many readers have failed to grasp this fact. For that matter, most editors have also been oblivious to the poem's visual appearance. In both the *Oeuvres complètes* and the current edition of *Clair de terre* (*Earthshine*), the text occupies the opposite sides of the same leaf.[9] The reader must turn the page to finish the poem, obscuring the visual image in the process. The latter does not portray just any vase, moreover, but one that is made of crystal. "As a hyperbole of *verre* (glass)," Michael Riffaterre notes, "*cristal* amplifies semes such as *transparence* [and] *fragility*."[10] Since Breton employs solid instead of outlined forms, the vase's transparency can only be imagined. The fact that it is fragile, however, is confirmed by its physical appearance. In addition, the word "crystal" conjures up visions of elegance. Since the vase is tall and graceful, it conforms to this prescription as well. It is not made of ordinary crystal, finally, but of the very best—crystal that comes from Bohemia. This last fact suggests that the vase is expensive.

Like Oliverio Girondo's scarecrow (see chapter 3), "Pièce fausse" is governed by two basic principles: repetition and redundancy. Fragments of each line are repeated over and over as the poem progresses. While Jean Gérard Lapacherie compares this phenomenon to stuttering, in reality it resembles a series of echoes.[11] It stems not from Breton's inability to express himself but from his decision to employ two complementary strategies, one visual, the other verbal. The phrases and bits of phrases make splendid building blocks, for example, with which to construct the visual image. In addition, they enable Breton to parody another genre in a different medium. Since the poem was published in *Dada,* one wonders initially if it wasn't simply a hoax—something designed to *épater la bourgeoisie.* Although this was undoubtedly one of its functions, sooner or later its main purpose dawns on the reader. "Pièce fausse" is meant to be a parody—a parody of an operatic aria.[12] The reason repetition plays such an important role, therefore, is because it has an operatic structure. After listening to Valéry Larbaud recite the work in Madrid in 1923, Guillermo de Torre praised its "inspiración burlesca."[13]

Breton may even have had a particular opera in mind. Internal evidence suggests that he sought to parody *La Bohème,* composed in 1896 by Giacomo Puccini. At the same time, another intriguing possibility exists. On May 26, 1920, during a Soirée Dada in the Salle Gaveau, Breton and Philippe Soupault performed their latest play, entitled *Vous m'oublierez* (*You Will Forget Me*). The third act of this nonsensical drama opened to the sound of someone singing "Pièce fausse" off-stage.[14] Fortunately, although the singer's identity remains a mystery, we have some idea what the song sounded like. According to a manuscript note, the music was borrowed from a famous aria in *Carmen:* "L'amour est enfant de bohême"

("Love is a child of Bohemia").[15] Sung by Carmen herself, alternating with the chorus, the aria appears in act I, scene 5 ("Habanera"):

> L'amour est enfant de bohème,
> Il n'a jamais jamais connu de loi,
> Si tu ne m'aimes pas, je t'aime;
> Si je t'aime, prends garde à toi.
>
> [Love is a child of Bohemia,
> It has never, never known a law,
> If you don't love me, I love you;
> If I love you, watch out.]

Although Breton could have composed "Pièce fausse" with the intention of parodying *Carmen,* this does not seem to have been the case. The idea of setting the work to Bizet's music apparently occurred to him when he was working on *Vous m'oublierez.* Unfortunately, as he presumably discovered, it is impossible to adapt the poem to the aria (or vice versa)—they are simply too dissimilar. The song must have sounded absolutely terrible, which, since it appeared in a Dada play, may have been exactly what Breton wanted. Interestingly, the Marx Brothers parodied the second half of the same scene in *A Night at the Opera* (1935). Something about "Habanera" just seems to call for parody.

At this point, it is useful to consider the poem's title: "Pièce fausse" ("False Piece"). As Lapacherie declares, "The title is indicative of Breton's satiric intentions. It constitutes a reading 'program' and encourages the reader to adopt a derisory interpretation."[16] Although "pièce" can designate a number of different objects, coupled with "fausse" it refers most obviously to a coin ("pièce de monnaie"). The fact that the latter is "false," however, means that it represents a counterfeit coin. And since money is not mentioned anywhere in the poem, it is clearly a metaphor for something else, something Breton feels is illegitimate. Lapacherie argues that the poem's scorn is directed at its own physical appearance and, by implication, at Apollinaire's calligrams. Instead of attempting to imitate painters, he adds, Breton believed poets should explore the possibilities of poetic language. As proof, he points out that "Pièce fausse" is composed of four octosyllabic verses rhyming ABAB:

> Du vase en cristal de Bohême
> Aux bulles qu'enfant tu soufflais

C'est là c'est là tout de poème
Aube éphémère de reflets

[From the crystal vase from Bohemia
To the bubbles as a child that you blew
There you have there you have the whole poem
Ephemeral dawn of reflections.]

Breton reduces the calligrams to a childish game, Lapacherie asserts, to soap bubbles blown by a bunch of children. Visual poetry is depicted as an illusion, as an ephemeral dawn of reflections.

Despite its radical appearance, "Pièce fausse" turns out to be surprisingly traditional at heart. As the editors of the Pléiade edition point out, the central quatrain was borrowed from an earlier poem entitled "Camaïeu" ("Cameo").[17] Written in 1914 during Breton's Symbolist period, it resembles a number of compositions by Mallarmé.[18] By 1920, when he created "Pièce fausse," Breton had embraced Dada and was on the brink of inventing Surrealism. Poetry itself had evolved to the point that it was no longer recognizable. Viewed from this vantage point, Breton's previous efforts must have seemed hopelessly old fashioned. Why, one wonders, did he decide to resurrect a poem from his earlier period? And why did he select this stanza instead of another one? Sooner or later the answer to the first question dawns on the reader. Breton chose "Camaïeu" precisely because the poem was so old fashioned. As it appears in "Pièce fausse," the stanza constitutes an object of derision. Breton deliberately mocks himself and his earliest poetry. The title reveals his satiric intentions, as Lapacherie says, but these are directed at the text rather than the visual image. The poem does not criticize Apollinaire's calligrams, therefore, but takes them as its point of departure.

Nevertheless, "Pièce fausse" is much more than an exercise in self-flagellation. Although Breton deplores his youthful folly, his derision is aimed primarily at another target. The reason he chose this particular stanza, to answer a previous question, is because it summarizes the Symbolist aesthetic. In contrast to the Parnassian poets, who equated poetry with sculpture, the Symbolists strove to capture fleeting impressions and delicate moods. Mallarmé advised his colleagues to "paint, not the thing, but the effect it produces."[19] Like the crystal vase in the first verse, the soap bubbles in the second symbolize delicate beauty. Unlike the vase, whose multiple facets sparkle with light, the bubbles only last for a moment. These two attributes—the play of light and the evanescence—reappear in the final verse: "Aube éphémère de reflets," which is auto-illustrative. The phrase simultaneously defines and represents Symbolist poetry. Ironically, as Louis Aragon observed, "Pièce fausse" represents "[a] break with obsolete poetic conventions."[20] Since Breton is denouncing the Symbolist enterprise, the verse is an example of how *not* to write poetry. Thus "Pièce fausse" turns out to contain two counterfeit coins: his early poetry and Symbolist aesthetics.

Pierre Albert-Birot

The most active practitioner of visual poetry during this period was neither a Dadaist nor a Surrealist but simply a member of the French avant-garde. The editor of a journal entitled *SIC* (*Sons, Idées, Couleurs*), which appeared from 1916 to 1919, Pierre Albert-Birot was a man of many talents. An active playwright, painter, and set designer, he also published numerous volumes of poetry. Although he was heavily influenced by Futurism, Cubism, and Dada, he managed to remain reasonably independent.[21] Instead of joining one of these movements, he founded a school of his own that he called Nunism after the Greek word for "now." Roughly equivalent to "modernism," his movement was thoroughly eclectic but seems to have attracted few if any disciples. While Albert-Birot failed to inspire any imitators, he served as an important avant-garde catalyst. Prefacing his first collection of poems in 1917, Apollinaire compared him to an arsonist because he ignited so many aesthetic fires.[22] With the publication of *La Joie des sept couleurs* (*The Joy of the Seven Colors*) two years later, his poetry finally came into its own. "A thirst for universality, for lyric communion dominates [this volume]," Jean Follain declares, "a thirst from which Albert-Birot will never deviate."[23] Among numerous traces of Apollinaire's influence, David Seaman adds, are several examples of visual poetry whose form and whimsical spirit recall the latter's calligrams.[24]

Albert-Birot had actually been writing visual poems for several years. Since there was no common term in use, he could never decide what to call them. Although he went on to create "poèmes-affiches" ("poster poems") and "poèmes-pancartes" ("placard-poems"), these terms did not become available until later. Faced with the same problem, Apollinaire was forced to invent a neologism: "calligramme." Uncertain how to respond, Albert-Birot employed a different terminology from one poem to the next. Appearing in *SIC* in December 1917, his first visual composition was entitled "Poème imagée" ("Imaged Poem"). Published the following year, the second and third examples were subtitled "poème idéogrammatique" and "poème-paysage" ("landscape poem"). While all three were visual poems, each was radically different from the others in inspiration as well as appearance. "Poème imagé," for example, also seems to have been conceived as a sound poem. Superimposed on either side of a curious drawing are two columns of words representing "deux voix simultanées" ["two simultaneous voices"] According to a note, readers are supposed to start at the bottom of the page and work their way to the top. The reason for this becomes clear as soon as one examines the drawing, which depicts several figures ascending to the top of a burning building. Who these individuals are, why they should be greeted by fire, and why the poem ends with a cat meowing is hard to say.

Published in *SIC* in April 1918, the second poem was entitled "Les Éclats" ("Shrapnel"). While "éclat" can designate a number of things, from a broken glass to a burst of laughter, the verbal ambiguity is reduced by the visual design. Seven lines of poetry extend upward in various directions from the horizontal like so many blades of grass. The fact that the poem was written during the First World War provides a helpful interpretive context. These are not blades of grass, one realizes, but splinters of a bursting artillery shell ("des éclats d'obus"). In order to decipher the composition, the reader must turn it clockwise ninety degrees, at which point it resembles a conventional poem.

> Je veux le coeur d'une vierge
> Je veux les seins d'une nourrice
> Pourquoi n'irais-je pas jusqu'à Dieu
> Je préfère un saint du paradis et des âmes en prière
> J'aurai un bras
> Moi je tuerai les pierres
> J'aurai une tête

> [I want a virgin's heart / I want a wet-nurse's breasts / Why wouldn't I turn to God / I prefer a saint in paradise and several souls at prayer / I will have an arm / I will kill the stones / I will have a head].

Unfortunately, this poem is nearly as enigmatic as the preceding one. Albert-Birot mentions four objects he would like to possess, two actions he would like to perform, and two value judgments. With a little rhetorical legerdemain, these can be converted into a list of eight objectives he would like to achieve. The question that arises at this point is why? What do saints, arms, and stones have in common that would justify this agenda? At first glance, the third and fourth lines suggest the poet is motivated by religious concerns. Perhaps he wants a virgin's heart in order to regain his lost innocence. However, nothing else in the poem supports this interpretation. Indeed, many verses don't even appear to make sense. Since Albert-Birot already has two arms, why does he need another one? Why does he need a second head? And what is he planning to do with two female breasts? The explanation seems to be that the second line is not spoken by the poet. In all probability, none of the lines are spoken by him. The poem was conceived not as a monologue but as a polyphony of different voices.

At this point, it becomes apparent that the visual design has not completely eliminated the verbal ambiguity. In retrospect, the work's title: "Les Éclats" turns out to involve a bit of wordplay. For if the visual composition depicts a bunch of shell splinters ("éclats d'obus"), as we saw previously, the verbal composition reproduces snatches of several conversations—several loud snatches ("éclats de voix"). Seven different characters insist on voicing their opinions. Since they all appear to be speaking at the same time, the scene is relatively chaotic. On a more general level, to be sure, the title evokes the cubist aesthetic underlying Albert-Birot's composition. Composed of seven "fragments" (another meaning of "éclats"), the poem is structured essentially like a collage. However, the title also refers to the human body parts mentioned in the poem. This realization reminds us of the central drama again and the fact that it takes place during World War I. Who are the speakers, one wonders, and how can they say such terrible things? Where are they anyhow, and what are they doing there? The explanation, when it finally dawns on the reader, is inescapable: the seven phrases are spoken by the exploding shell fragments. The first fragment boasts that it will kill a young girl, the second that it will disfigure a wet-nurse, the third and fourth that they will reach the saints in heaven, the fifth that it will slice off an arm, the sixth that it will destroy a building, and the seventh that it will decapitate someone.

Reviewing "Les Éclats" for inclusion in *La Lune* six years later, Albert-Birot decided that two things needed to be changed.[25] The first modification was relatively minor and involved the poem's appearance. Grouping the vertical lines together, he rearranged them in a fan-shaped pattern. Compared to those in the earlier version, they were more concentrated, more focused, and presumably more dangerous. The second modification was much more substantial. Responding to the barrage of shell fragments, which threatened to harm innocent civilians, Albert-Birot added the following words at the upper left: "Je / t' / ai / me" ["I / lo / ve / you."] As Debra Kelly remarks, these words contain a powerful message of love and hope.[26] Presumably uttered by the Creator, they encourage humanity not to despair. The fact that they are curved like a rainbow reminds the viewer of the covenant between heaven and earth.

Published in May 1918, the third visual composition that appeared in *SIC* was entitled "Poème-Paysage" ("Landscape Poem"). Despite the description provided by the title, very little of the landscape is actually visible. The foreground is occupied by two objects that prevent us from seeing anything else: a large house and a tall tree. Since the tree reaches all the way to the top of the page, its branches block out whatever is not obscured by the building. "**In the background,**" a note at the upper left informs us, "**There is the sea / And behind the sea / There are other houses.**" Masquerading as a banal description, this curious statement poses more questions than it answers. While there are undoubtedly houses on the other side of the sea, how can the speaker possibly see them? They would normally be too far away. And if he or she can't see the houses,

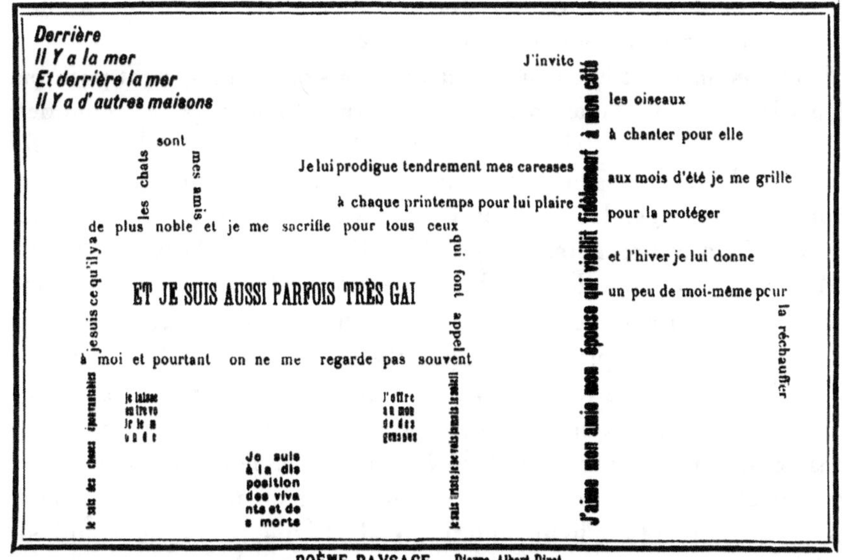

12. Pierre Albert-Birot, "Poème-Paysage"

why mention them in the first place? The perspective is troubling in other respects as well. While the speaker stresses the depth of field, for example, which extends all the way across the sea, the visual design is limited to two dimensions. For all practical purposes, it coincides with the picture plane. Nothing exists behind the house, because there simply is no place to put it.

To judge by the rooftop, the chimney, and the two rooms, the picture presents a side view of the house. Deciphering the words that make up the building is an awkward experience at best. The reader must continually turn the page this way and that in order to puzzle out the poem's meaning. The most fruitful approach seems to be to rotate the page clockwise ninety degrees. Beginning at the upper left, one reads the phrase: "I know some terrible things" followed by the parallel phrase (in the same typeface) at the bottom: "I am sad. I never see the sun." Although the first statement makes little sense, the second statement is crystal clear. Since the rear wall of the house is shaded by the tree, it is protected from the sunlight. Returning to the top of the page, the reader deciphers the topmost edge of the roof (in reality the left side) and then the other three edges, rotating the poem as necessary. This operation produces the following sentence: "There is something very noble / about me, and I sacrifice myself for all those / who call on me, and yet no one looks at me very often." Like so many other utilitarian objects, the house is taken for granted by those who live in it. The only time it receives any attention is when it needs a coat of paint or a new roof.

By this time, the house has returned to its original, upright position. This is as good a time as any to read the chimney, which confides: "The cats / are / my friends." Presumably it is also visited by playful birds and squirrels. The remaining features can be deciphered without rotating the page. Despite the house's occasional sadness, a banner across the roof proclaims: "AND SOMETIMES I AM ALSO VERY MERRY." Unlike the left window, which describes what people can see from inside: "I allow people to glimpse the world," the right window describes what people can see from the outside looking in: "I present naked people to the world." Whereas the first window belongs to the front room, the second window clearly looks into a bedroom, whose residents often forget to pull down the shade. This leaves the door, sandwiched in between the two windows, which announces: "I am at the disposition of the living and the dead." Living people go in and out all the time. When they eventually die, they are carried out of the house feet first.

Deciphering the tree standing next to the house is a more straightforward process. All it requires is a ninety degree turn to the right and two turns in the opposite direction to unlock its message. The first operation exposes the trunk to view. Since it is much wider and darker than the branches, Albert-Birot employs a larger, boldface font. The first line introduces a charming conceit: "**I love my sweetheart my faithful wife who grows old beside me**." Like a human couple gradually aging together, the house and the tree are sustained by their love for each other. Returning the poem to its original position, we are immediately faced with a choice. We can begin with the word at the top of the page ("J'invite") or the word at the extreme left ("Je"), but not both. The second strategy, which divides the poem into two columns, provides the following reading: "I cover her with tender kisses / every spring to give her pleasure / I invite / the birds / to sing for her / I burn myself to a crisp in the summer / to protect her / and in the winter I give her / a little of myself / to keep her warm." Continuing the extended metaphor, the poet translates the tree's spring foliage brushing against the house's roof into a gesture of affection. Shading the house from the fierce sun, the tree adopts a protective role in the summer—an overprotective role, as it turns out. Not only is the house unappreciative, but she finds the constant lack of sunshine depressing. When November arrives, however, the tree contributes dead branches (one of which is hanging from the last line) for the house to burn in her fireplace. Secure in the knowledge that his companion is warm, he stoically endures winter's icy blasts.

"Poème imagé" was never collected in any of Albert-Birot's subsequent books, perhaps because he felt it was too arcane. "Poème-Paysage" was published in *La Joie des sept couleurs* the following year and "Les Éclats" in *La Lune* five years later. The first volume contained a number of other visual poems as well. One of the more interesting examples depicts a locomotive and a passenger car standing in a railroad station. Like "Poème-Paysage," it is surrounded by an elaborate frame, which emphasizes its status as a pictorial artifact. Although the title appears to be "**L'HEURE**" ("**THE HOUR**"), as David Seaman notes, the original composition was probably entitled "Poème-Paysage"—like the poem examined previously.[27] When Albert-Birot collected the two works in a single volume, he simply eliminated their titles (which were purely generic). While "**L'HEURE**" functions as the composition's de facto title, this role was imposed upon it by later events. In reality, it represents the large clock that was the central fixture of every railroad station. Among other things, the scene recalls Claude Monet's paintings of the Gare Saint-

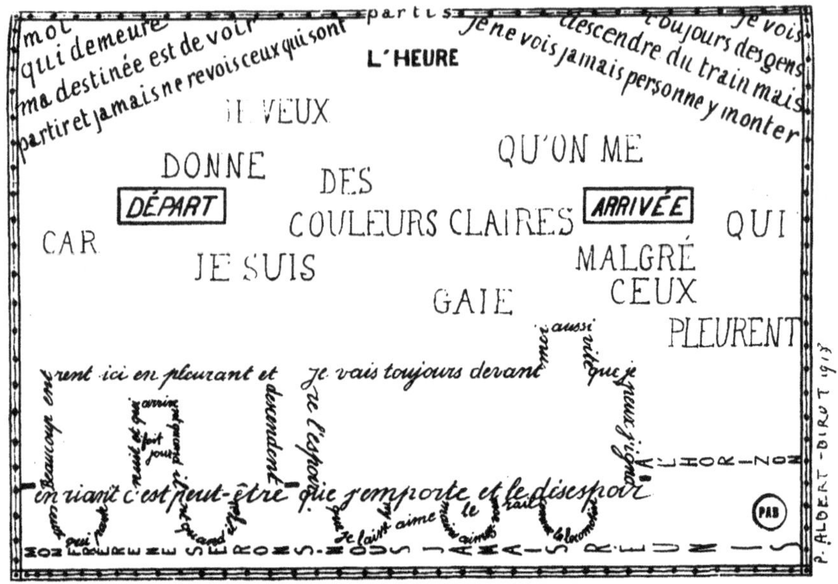

13. **Pierre Albert-Birot, "L'HEURE"**

Lazare in Paris. At the top of the page, four diagonal lines of text on either side represent the station's peaked roof.

I / who remain / my destiny is to see / those who have left and to never see them / again	I always / see people / getting off the train but / I never see anyone getting on

THE HOUR

I WOULD LIKE TO HAVE SOME PALE COLORS

DEPARTURE	**ARRIVAL**

I AM GAY DESPITE THOSE WHO ARE CRYING

Since the roof beams are situated on opposite sides of the station, their perspective is severely limited. Those on the left see only passengers who are leaving, and those on the right, passengers who are arriving. Inevitably, each experience is destined to be incomplete. Seaman assumes the words in large capitals in the middle of the page are spoken by "**L'HEURE.**"[28] However, it seems to be the station itself that is actually speaking. Perhaps because it is gay at heart, the building yearns to be redecorated in pastel shades. That people are crying comes as a bit of a surprise until one examines the composition more closely. Since the passenger car is stationed in front of the departure sign, the train must be preparing to leave. As the time to depart approaches, the air is filled with sudden tears and emotional goodbyes. Deciphering the train itself, which is outlined in cursive script, poses a series of new problems. The complicated visual demands placed on the poet by the composition (and vice versa) ensured that little attention would be paid to its verbal requirements. Although a correct reading strategy does exist, it violates the reader's expectations at every turn. The only way to proceed is through trial and error.

The first problem that confronts the reader is deciding where to begin. Although it is tempting to tackle the passenger car first, since it is on the left, the larger capital that begins the locomotive's message signals this as the place to start. Since the locomotive pulls the rest of the train, this strategy makes perfectly good sense. The reader proceeds in a clockwise direction, rotating the page to the left or the right as necessary. While the transition between the top of the drawing and its right side is relatively smooth, the message suddenly breaks off. Casting around for the missing fragment, one discovers that it constitutes the figure's left side. Thereafter, the reader performs the same operation on the passenger car, which differs from the locomotive in one important respect. Its lower edge extends all the way across the page, forming the locomotive's lower edge as well. The poet adopts a smaller font for the remainder of the train, which makes it harder to read. Proceeding from left to right, one deciphers the passenger car's left wheel, the door, the right wheel, and each of the wheels belonging to the locomotive. The last three words form a primitive connecting rod joining the latter's wheels together. Despite a few grammatical irregularities, the text reads as follows:

I go straight ahead as fast as I / can I igno / re
    hope
  Many people en / ter crying and / exit / laughing
    perhaps I take it and despair away
those who depart at night and arrive when it is day
I leave you to your destiny
love each other as the locomotive loves the rails.

The first message is uttered by the locomotive, which is proud of its tremendous power and speed. Oblivious to human distractions such as love and hope, it eagerly plunges ahead, determined to reach its destination. The second message is uttered by the passenger car, which is proud of the security and comfort it offers. By the end of the journey, the tearful goodbyes have been forgotten and the passengers are thoroughly enjoying themselves. Travel by train is not only pleasurable, the speaker observes, but positively therapeutic. The last three lines are addressed to passengers traveling at night, whom, for some reason, Albert-Birot enjoins to love each other. On the one hand, he may be thinking of lovers running off together to start a new life. On the other, he may be referring to people traveling overnight to visit loved ones. Stretching "TO THE HORIZON," the rails at the bottom of the page echo the poet's own thoughts: "MY BROTHER WILL WE NEVER SEE EACH OTHER AGAIN [?]"

Two of the visual poems in *La Lune* were occasioned by Apollinaire's tragic death, which profoundly affected the avant-garde. Since Albert-Birot had worked so closely with him, his personal sense of loss was especially great. Entitled "**POÈME AU MORT**" ("**POEM TO THE DECEASED**") in heavy boldface letters, the first composition depicts the poet's funeral at the Église Saint-Thomas-d'Aquin on November 13, 1918. Resting on a massive bier, Apollinaire's coffin is crowned by three photographs draped in black crepe and flanked by two large funerary wreaths.

IS IT AN END OR A BEGINNING

FOR
GUILLAUME APOLLINAIRE
THE POETS

A

FOR
GUILLAUME APOLLINAIRE
THE FLOWERS

G **K**

Light is the Poet's sister
Light is the Poet's wife
Light is the Poet's form
Light is the Poet's breath
The Poet the Poet is Light

I AM BLACK AND BLACK
CAUSES PEOPLE TO CRY I AM
HATED BY MANKIND ALL I KNOW OF MANKIND IS
TEARS AND SOBS I SPEND MY LIFE IN CHURCHES THOSE SILENT
RAILROAD STATIONS FROM WHICH TRAINS LEAVE FOR HEAVEN MEN DO
NOT BE AFRAID OF ME DO NOT HATE ME WHEN YOU REST ON ME YOU ARE
HIGHER THAN EVERYONE I AM A PEDESTAL A BLACK PEDESTAL TRUE
BUT FROM WHICH ONE SEES FAR Ô IF YOU KNEW HOW FAR WHEN ONE RESTS
ON ME Ô IF YOU KNEW MANKIND WHO LOVE TO GAZE FAR OFF DO NOT
FEAR BLACK THE INVISIBLE TRAINS LEAVE FOR HEAVEN EVERY SECOND
GET ON STRETCH OUT THEY ARE SLEEPING CARS I AM THE PLATFORM I AM
BLACK I AM BLACK THERE IS A LONG LONG TUNNEL LIKE DESPAIR BUT IT
OPENS INTO BRIGHT LIGHT WHERE GUILLAUME APOLLINAIRE JUST ARRIVED

FRIENDS MY FRIENDS HOW BEAUTIFUL INFINITY IS
WE ARE CIRCUMFERENCES

POÈME AU MORT

EST-CE UNE FIN OU UN COMMENCEMENT

A

G

La Lumière est la sœur du Poète
La Lumière est l'épouse du Poète
La Lumière est la femme du Poète
La Lumière est le souffle du Poète
Le Poète le Poète est la Lumière

JE SUIS NOIR ET LE NOIR
FAIT PLEURER LES HOMMES JE SUIS
HAÏ DES HOMMES JE NE CONNAIS DES HOMMES QUE LES
PLEURS ET LES SANGLOTS JE PASSE MA VIE DANS LES ÉGLISES CES GARES
SILENCIEUSES D'OU LES TRAINS PARTENT POUR LE CIEL HOMMES N'AYEZ PAS
PEUR DE MOI NE ME HAÏSSEZ PAS QUAND VOUS ÊTES COUCHÉS SUR MOI VOUS ÊTES PLUS
HAUT QUE LES AUTRES JE SUIS UN PIÉDESTAL UN PIÉDESTAL NOIR IL EST VRAI MAIS D'OU
L'ON VOIT DE HAUT O SI VOUS SAVIEZ COMME L'ON VOIT DE HAUT QUAND ON EST COUCHÉ
SUR MOI O SI VOUS SAVIEZ VOUS LES HOMMES QUI AIMEZ TANT A VOIR DE HAUT N'AYEZ
PAS PEUR DU NOIR LES TRAINS INVISIBLES PARTENT POUR LE CIEL TOUTES LES SECONDES
MONTEZ ÉTENDEZ-VOUS CE SONT DES SLEEPING-CARS JE SUIS LE QUAI DE DÉPART JE SUIS
NOIR JE SUIS NOIR C'EST UN LONG LONG TUNNEL COMME LE DÉSESPOIR MAIS IL DÉBOU-
CHE • DANS • LA • CLARTÉ • OU • VIENT • D'ARRIVER • GUILLAUME • APOLLINAIRE

MES AMIS MES AMIS COMME EST BEAU L'INFINI

NOUS SOMMES DES CIRCONFÉRENCES

14. Pierre Albert-Birot, “POÈME AU MORT”

The poem begins with the question that traditionally arises at funerals —is there life after death? Does death represent the end of all our dreams, or is it a threshold to a glorious new experience? The fact that Albert-Birot asks this question at all reveals he is reluctant to accept Catholic dogma. For the moment, in any event, the question evokes no response. At first glance, the wreath on the left seems to have been sent by Apollinaire's fellow poets, whose collective name appears at the bottom. By the same logic, however, one would expect the right-hand wreath to have been sent by the flowers, whose name also appears at the bottom. In retrospect, one perceives that the wreaths implicitly function as visual metaphors. They signify (1) that numerous poets have come to pay tribute to Apollinaire and (2) that the church is filled with flowers. Representing pictures of the deceased poet, the letters **G A K** stand for Guillaume Apollinaire de Kostrowitzky. Beneath the pictures, a rectangular block composed of five lines of poetry constitutes the poet's coffin. These are arranged to form a litany, during the course of which Apollinaire is progressively transformed into Light. By the end of the poem, when his apotheosis is complete, he has become a divine principle. Whether this symbol was chosen consciously or unconsciously, it dovetails nicely with Apollinaire's own symbolism. "J'aime l'art d'aujourd'hui," he explained in *Méditation esthétiques,* "parce que j'aime avant tout la lumière" ["I love today's art because I love light above all else"].[29]

As we have had ample opportunity to observe, objects in Albert-Birot's poetry often possess a voice. As soon as the litany is finished, for example, the bier pronounces a long, impassioned speech, much of which is basically irrelevant. Whereas the poem is supposedly concerned with Apollinaire, the bier complains about its own lot in life. Confined to the dark recesses of the church, it emerges periodically to encounter people who are crying and sobbing. Universally feared and detested, the bier protests that it deserves to be viewed more favorably. Those who lie atop its platform, for example, are treated to an incredible view—presumably encompassing all of existence. If the bier bears a certain resemblance to Mt. Everest, the church in which it stands resembles a railroad station. According to the speaker, invisible trains depart every second carrying newly liberated souls to heaven. Just when it seems the journey will never end, they emerge from a long tunnel into the dazzling light, where Apollinaire is waiting to welcome them. The poem concludes with two observations. Once death is conceived as an encounter with the infinite, the poet announces, it becomes a beautiful experience. Unlike Pascal, who was terrified by the thought of infinity, he finds it exhilarating. Returning to the question posed at the beginning, Albert-Birot refuses to consider death as either an end or a beginning. Since existence is circular, it simply represents a transition.

Entitled "Offrande" ("Offering"), the second poem was composed a few years later while Albert-Birot was vacationing in Monaco. Recalling that Apollinaire spent much of his childhood there, he decided to create

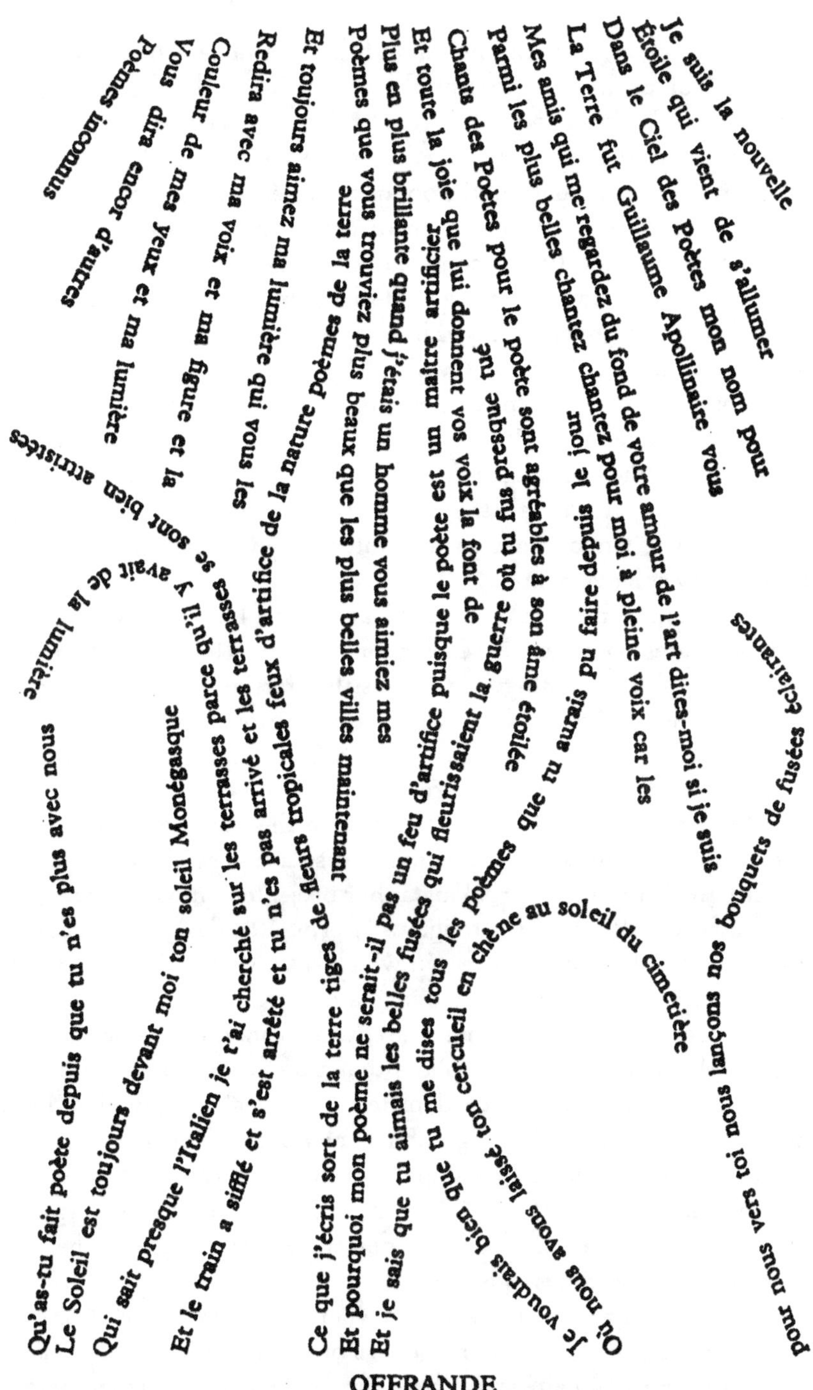

15. Pierre Albert-Birot, "Offrande"

a visual dialogue between himself and the poet in heaven. This explains why the composition is structured vertically and why it is divided into two halves. The lower portion is reserved for Albert-Birot, whose words ascend toward the top of the page, and the upper portion for Apollinaire, whose response descends in the opposite direction. The first message requires a quarter turn to the right to decipher; the second message, a half turn to the left. For various reasons, Albert-Birot insisted on publishing most of his works himself. Besides the obvious financial advantages, this arrangement allowed him to retain complete control over his artistic production. And since he did all his own printing, he soon became an accomplished typographer. Some of the visual compositions, such as "Poème-Paysage" and "Poème au mort," adhere to the traditional rectilinear grid. Other compositions, such as "Les Éclats" and "Offrande," defy any attempt to contain them. This describes the second poem in particular, whose sinuous design and intertwined lines represent an extraordinary achievement.

In addition to being a typographical tour de force, the visual design communicates on several levels simultaneously. The recognition that it constitutes a visual dialogue serves as the starting point. Since spoken words are not really visible, however, the picture at this level is entirely imaginary. The verbal exchange between Albert-Birot and Apollinaire is rendered schematically. At the realistic level, by contrast, several other possibilities exist. As the poet notes during the course of the poem, the composition resembles a pyrotechnical display. Viewed from this angle, the design represents a verbal metaphor projected onto the visual plane. And since an "offrande" is a religious offering, the design could conceivably depict a cloud of incense—in which case, it would also be a visual metonym. Whereas these figures play a relatively minor role, two additional images exist that dominate the entire poem. Like the pyrotechnics, both of them are verbal metaphors that have been raised to the visual level. Albert-Birot's words are depicted as tropical vegetation and Apollinaire's words as rays of sunlight. Each metaphor complements the other and comments on the relationship between the two poets. Just as plants derive energy from sunlight, Albert-Birot's poetry derives its inspiration from Apollinaire's example. Like tropical flowers basking in the sun, it absorbs his radiant message.

Looming over the rest of the poem, where they serve as vivid emblems, these two images illuminate the poem's broader concerns. The relationship between Apollinaire and Albert-Birot is clearly that of mentor to disciple. The ultimate *offrande* is the poem itself, which the latter presents to his beloved master. Filled with poignant memories, it is by turns affectionate, witty, and sad.

> What have you been doing poet since you left us
> Your sun is still here in Monaco
> It almost knows Italian I looked for you on the terraces because they
> were full of light
> And the train whistled and stopped and you didn't get off and the terraces
> grew very sad
> What I am writing comes from the earth stems of tropical flowers
> fireworks from nature poems from the earth
> Why couldn't my poem be a firework since poets are fired with
> enthusiasm
> And I know you loved the beautiful flares that bloomed during the
> war in which you were nearly killed
> I would like you to tell me all the poems you have made since the day
> We left your oak coffin in the cemetery's sun
> for us toward you we throw our bouquets of signal flares.

As in the previous poem, and for similar reasons, Albert-Birot portrays Apollinaire as the poet of light. Whereas light is related to divine revelation in "**POÈME AU MORT,**" it is associated here, as we have seen, with the emblematic sun. Since Monaco is near Italy, the poet jokes that the sun speaks broken Italian. The association between Apollinaire and light was so fixed in his mind, he adds, that he found himself looking for the poet on the sunny terraces. Similarly, since Apollinaire grew up in Monaco, he half expected to see him get off the train. Comparing the poem to tropical flowers and fireworks ("feux d'artifice"), Albert-Birot engages in a bit of wordplay. The second comparison is justified, he insists, because every poet is a master of artifice. In any case, he adds, Apollinaire himself admired the signal flares when he was fighting at the front. "Que c'est beau ces fusées qui illuminent la nuit," . . . he exclaimed in one poem, "Ce sont des dames qui dansent avec leurs regards pour yeux bras et coeurs" ["How beautiful these flares are illuminating the night . . . They are ladies who dance with their gaze instead of their eyes arms and hearts"].[30] Now that the war is over, Albert-Birot confides, he would love to know what the poet has been writing about in heaven. Transforming the preceding message into a bouquet of flares, he launches them in Apollinaire's direction.

Observing the scene from his celestial abode, Apollinaire responds with a message of his own. Since he is the poet of light, his words are concerned with the principle that animates him.

I am the new
Star that has just begun to shine
In the Poets' Sky my name on
Earth was Guillaume Apollinaire you
My friends who gaze at me from the depth of your love of art tell me if I am one of the lovelier ones sing sing loudly for me for the
Songs of the Poets please the poet's starry soul
And all the joy your voices give him make it
Brighter and brighter when I was a man you loved my
Poems which you found more beautiful than the most beautiful cities now
Continue to love my light which will
Tell them to you again with my voice and my face and the
Color of my eyes and my light
Will tell you more
Unknown poems

While Apollinaire's speech is not devoid of interest, it catches the reader totally by surprise. Not only is there is no trace of the visual dialogue between him and Albert-Birot, but it appears to contradict that dialogue. Although the visual image occupying the top half of the page clearly represents sunlight, Apollinaire declares that he is a star—a brand new star in the poetic firmament. At the purely verbal level, this statement makes perfectly good sense. Apollinaire is portrayed as a stellar poet—as a beacon shining in the wilderness. The reader imagines a night sky populated by former poets who have been transformed into celestial bodies. Where the problem arises is when one attempts to translate it onto the visual plane. The idea of tropical plants deriving energy from starlight is frankly ludicrous. A serious conflict exists as well between the two speeches, which supposedly constitute a dialogue. What looks like a response on Apollinaire's part is not a response at all. Instead of replying to Albert-Birot's affectionate greetings, he addresses his friends in general. However, the message he sends them is far from inspiring. Apollinaire first asks if his star is beautiful. Then he commands his friends to sing his praises, so his star will shine more brightly. Instead of offering words of wisdom, all he seems to care about is his posthumous reputation. Ironically, although the poem was originally conceived as a homage to Apollinaire, it portrays him in an unflattering light. To be sure, this is no reflection on the latter but rather on Albert-Birot, who failed to realize there was a problem.

5
Italian Futurist Aeropoetry

ON SEPTEMBER 22, 1929, F. T. MARINETTI PUBLISHED A DOCUMENT that would profoundly affect the nature of Futurist research: the *Manifesto of Futurist Aeropainting.*[1] In particular, he urged the Futurist painters to celebrate "the immense visual and sensory drama of flight." The artists responded enthusiastically to Marinetti's challenge and produced a series of paintings that are as striking today as when they were originally created.[2] Inspired by the latter, other individuals began to experiment with aerial aesthetics as well, including the Futurist writers. In 1931, Marinetti published a *Manifesto of Futurist Aeropoetry,* in which he encouraged the Futurist poets to emulate the aeropainters.[3] During the next thirteen years, he and his colleagues celebrated the triumph of modern aviation in poem after poem. Evoking the physical and psychological sensation of flying, they described what they saw, what they experienced, and how it affected them. Curiously, despite the Futurist poets' longstanding commitment to visual effects, Marinetti insisted that radio was the best vehicle for aeropoetry. This undoubtedly explains why there are relatively few aeropoems that also function as visual poems. In theory at least, aeropoetry was meant to be heard and not seen.

Ignazio Scurto

Despite Marinetti's comments, a number of aeropoets occasionally experimented with visual poetry. One of the first poets to explore the possibilities of this hybrid form was Ignazio Scurto, who belonged to the Gruppo Futurista Boccioni in Verona. Claudia Salaris calls him the most interesting writer of the whole group.[4] In 1932, he published the following poem in *Futurismo,* edited in Rome by Mino Semenzi.[5]

V O L O
S U
T R A Ú
(a e r o p o e s i a)
volare sui tubi infiam
mati del sole cromo
alluminio amplifica
tori del mio saluto
3000 HP Fiat all'in
sopprimibile
diritto
biancorosso
verde delle
generazioni
d a l m a t e
m o t o r e s u c c h i a r e
dalle mie vene che
c o n t e n g o n o t u t t o
l' a d r i a t i c o
l'incontenibile ruggi
to contro i
MERCANTI
DI PORCI
t r a m u t a n d o l o n e l
suo rombo italianis
simo
TRAÚ
TRAÚTRAÚ
TRAÚTRAÚTRAÚ
TRAÚTRAÚTRAÚTRAÚ
TRAÚTRAÚTRAÚTRAÚ
raccolto religio
samente dai C
A
M
PA
NI
LI

veneti che sguscia
no verso di me cer
cando di avvinghiar
si alla mia carlinga
fascista
QUANDO?
campane sonorizza
re grida dalmate in
occasione del pas
saggio in cielo del
futurista - dalmata
SCURTO
QUANDDDD DOdo
QUAND ND DO?
TRAÚTRAÚTRAÚTRAÚ
TRAÚ TRAÚ
1933
TRAÚTRAÚTRAÚTRAÚ

[FLIGHT
OV ER
TROGIR
(aeropoem)
flying over pipes lit
by the sun chrome
aluminum amplifi
ers of my greeting
3000 HP Fiat with the
irrepressible
r e d w h i te
g r e e n
C l a i m
of dalmatian
generations
motor drawing an
irresistible roar from
my veins which con

tain the entire
a d r i a t i c
directed against the
HOG
BUTCHERS
transforming it into
a t o t a l l y i t a l
ian throbbing
TRAÚ
TRAÚTRAÚ
TRAÚTRAÚTRAÚ
TRAÚTRAÚTRAÚTRAÚ
TRAÚTRAÚTRAÚTRAÚ
carefully gathered
from the venetian T
O
W
E
R
S
—

w h i c h r e a c h
t o w a r d m e s e e k
i n g t o c l i n g t o
m y f a s c i s t
cockpit
W H E N ?
d a l m a t i a n b e l l s
c e l e b r a t i n g t h e
celestial passage of the
dalmatian - futurist
SCURTO
WHEEEE EN EN EN
WHEN NNN NN?
TRAÚTRAÚTRAÚTRAÚ
TRAÚ TRAÚ
1933
TRAÚTRAÚTRAÚTRAÚ].

Flying over the Dalmatian port of Trogir (Traù in Italian), Scurto hears church bells ringing and observes his airplane's reflection in the shiny metal structures below. Responding to what he fondly imagines to be the town's greeting, he dips his wings in a quick salute. Since Scurto was born and raised in Verona, one wonders how he could possibly claim to be a Dalmatian Futurist. Eventually one perceives that he is speaking not as an individual but in his capacity as an Italian citizen. Like the Adriatic, which pulses in his veins, Trogir belongs to Scurto because it belongs to Italy—represented by the red, white, and green flag. Between 1420 and 1797, the town was part of the former Venetian empire. Among the important buildings that survive from this period are several Renaissance churches, whose prominent bell towers are evoked in the poem. Dissolving the word "CAMPANILI" into its individual letters, Scurto arranges them vertically to create a visual analogy. The latter not only designates the object in question but depicts it as well. Elsewhere he employs a series of ascending or descending fonts to indicate that a sound is getting louder or softer. As the poem concludes, Scurto makes one last pass over the town. We hear the airplane approaching initially: "TRAÚTRAÚTRAÚTRAÚ," and then we hear it flying away: "TRAÚTRAÚTRAÚTRAÚ."

While most of the poem's visual effects are easy to decipher, one feature is frankly puzzling. For some reason, the text is compressed into a narrow ribbon that is justified on both sides. Why, one wonders, did Scurto choose such an unusual shape? Why is the poem so long and thin? Although it is tempting to conclude that it represents one of the bell towers, a rapid review reveals they all have pointed roofs. For that matter, why did the poet choose such huge letters for the poem's title? And why are they arranged to form a rectangle? All of a sudden, the pieces of the puzzle begin to fall into place. The title represents Kamerlengo Castle, constructed by the Venetians in the fifteenth century. The remainder of the poem depicts Trogir's main street, which stretches from the castle to the other side of the town. Rising over the middle of Trogir is St. Mark's Tower, which also dates from the fifteenth century.

While "VOLO SU TRAÚ" recounts a personal experience (or purports to), it also dramatizes Italy's desire to annex the Dalmatian coast. However, Scurto is not simply asserting Italy's right to reacquire former lands. He is thinking of the Treaty of London (1915), which promised to cede Northern Dalmatia and other territories to Italy in exchange for joining the Allies during World War I. Although this promise was forgotten after the war, Scurto insists that Italy has a legitimate claim ("diritto") to occupy Trogir. Indeed, he declares, the Christian population would welcome such a move, since the Muslim invaders (vilified as "MERCANTI DI PORCI") would be expelled. Amid a flurry of rhetorical questions in ascending fonts, the poem concludes on a militant note. Insisting that the time is ripe, Scurto urges the Italian government to occupy Trogir by next year (1933).

Pino Masnata

Pino Masnata joined the Futurist movement at an early age, made a number of important contributions, and eventually became a surgeon. Born and raised in Stradella (between Pavia and Piacenza), he published a collection of plays in 1930, a book of poetry in 1932, and, together with Marinetti, a *Manifesto futurista della radio* in 1933. Entitled *Tavole parolibere* (*Free-Word Paintings*), the second volume revolutionized the practice of visual poetry. "Pino Masnata's free-word poetry," Marinetti declared in the introduction, "is original, expressive, aggressive, condensed and yet freely flowing like a sheet of ice in the sun."[6] The following year, Masnata decided to combine his interest in visual poetry with the recently invented genre of *aeropoesia*. Like Ignazio Scurto before him, he chose to publish his first attempt in *Futurismo*.[7] Entitled "**AEROPLANI**," the composition was, in his own words, "a long free-word painting celebrating aviation with squadrons of Ts in formation."[8]

A I R P L A N E S

AIRPLANES ROAR FLYING SQUADRONS

r r r r r r r r r r r r r r

what are all of them saying

T?

The peaceful man Tedium

Turbulence Tax

Topsy-turvy Turmoil

The painter Titian

Table cloth Tablet

Tint or else Tapestry

AEROPLANI

ROMBO DI AEROPLANI IN VOLO SQUADRIGLIE

r r r r r r r r r r r r r r r r r r r r r

cosa vogliono dire tutte quelle

T ?

Il pacifico **Turbamento Tedio Tassa**
Tramescolamento o meglio Trambusto

Il pittore **Tappeto Tiziano Tavolozza**
Tinta o meglio Tappezzeria

Il commerciante **Trasferimento Trasloco Trasporto**
Tariffa o meglio Traffico

L'anti-italiano **Tranello Tana Trucco**
Tradimento o meglio Tormento

Il medico **Trachea Tibia Tendine**
Tricuspide o meglio Termocauterio

L'avvocato **Tribunale Toga Truffa**
Testamento o meglio Tutela

L'operaio **Tecnica Tela Tubo**
Traliccio o meglio Trivella

Il vile **Tragedia Tremito Terra**
Tremarella o meglio Tomba

Il poeta passatista **Tersicore Talia Tomi**
Tipografia o meglio Tantalo

Il musicista **Tastiera Tocco Tromba**
Tono o meglio Trio

Il matematico **Trigonometria Tangente Trapezio**
Trapezoide o meglio Triangolo

Il botanico **Tolù Tiglio Timo**
Tulipano o meglio Trifoglio

L'ecclesiastico **Teologia Tonaca Talare**
Temporale o meglio Trinità

La donna **Taffetà Trina Talamo**
Tesoro o meglio Tenerezza

Il militare **Truppa Traino Treno**
Trabocchetto o meglio Tattica

Il futurista e fascista **Tonnellata Torma Tonfo**
Terrore o meglio Trionfo

o meglio ancora Traù

16. Pino Masnata, "AEROPLANI"

The merchant Transfer
Transference Transport
Tariff or else Traffic

The anti-Italian Tunnel
Trap Trick
Treachery or else Torment

The doctor Tibia
Trachea Tendon
Triscuspid or else Thermocautery

The lawyer Toga
Tribunal Trickery
Testament or else Tutelage

The worker Towel
Technique Tube
Trellis-work or else Tool

The coward Tremble
Tragedy Terra
Tremors or else Tomb

The obsolete poet Thalia
Terpsichore Tomes
Typography or else Tantalus

The musician Touch
The ivories Trumpet
Tone or else Trio

The mathematician Tangent
Trigonometry Trapezium
Trapezoid or else Triangle

The botanist Tea
Tolu balsam Thyme
Tulip or else Trefoil

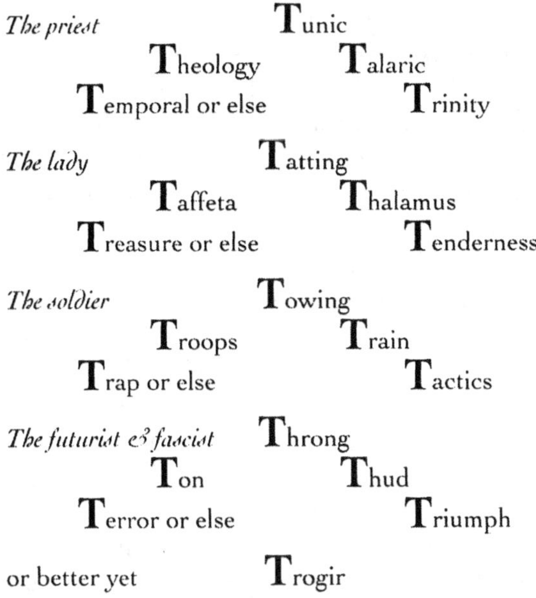

Despite its relative simplicity, Masnata's visual design is extraordinarily effective. As wave after wave of airplanes sweeps by overhead, the viewer gazes in amazement. The cumulative effect is almost hypnotic. Flying in a series of V formations are eighty-two planes divided into sixteen squadrons. Contributing to the realistic effect, the capital Ts at the beginning of each word are shaped like airplanes. Although the aircraft in question have no insignia, they clearly belong to the Italian air force. In spite of Masnata's previous claim, the composition does not celebrate aviation in general but rather *Italian* aviation, which was attracting considerable attention. In December 1930, the Italian air minister Italo Balbo led a group of twelve Savoia-Marchetti S.55 flying boats from their base at Orbetello to Rio de Janeiro. Like the airplanes in Masnata's composition, they flew the entire distance in military formation. Balbo performed a similar exploit two and a half years later, commanding twenty-four seaplanes on a round-trip flight to Chicago, where he received a hero's welcome. Chicago named a street after him, New York held a ticker-tape parade in his honor, and President Roosevelt invited him to lunch. As a result of this adventure, the expression "balbo" was coined in Italian to describe a large formation of aircraft.[9]

Since "**AEROPLANI**" is composed entirely of nouns, whether it qualifies as a poem is open to dispute. Although Marinetti advocated the abolition of adverbs and adjectives, he recommended the use of verbs in the infinitive.[10] As we saw previously, Masnata viewed it as a free-word painting. Regardless of what one chooses to call this intriguing work, it occupies a unique place in the Futurist canon. Evoking Italian citizens from every walk of life, it portrays the Italian air force as the pride and joy of the entire nation. Each squadron is identified with a different kind of person, who evokes five things associated with his or her existence. Some individuals are worthy of praise, and some are not. While the Futurists admired painters, musicians, and soldiers, for example, they despised cowards, anti-Italians, and obsolete poets. The first three individuals are juxtaposed with objects, concepts, or people related to their professions. Personified by Titian, the artist utilizes a palette, the musician plays an instrument, and the soldier employs clever tactics.

Unlike the coward and the anti-Italian in the group, who tend to be defined by their personal characteristics, the obsolete poet espouses outmoded concepts. Whereas the former tremble uncontrollably or engage in treacherous acts, the latter reveres the nine muses. Like Tantalus, he attempts to steal nectar and ambrosia from the gods. Influenced perhaps by Marinetti, who encouraged poets to write for the radio, Masnata includes typography among the list of obsolete practices. Since Futurist poetry was famous for its typographical effects, this is rather surprising. One wonders if the present composition is also outmoded, since it could never be transmitted via radio. In condemning typography, Masnata has unwittingly endangered his own enterprise as well. The front of the airborne formation is occupied by the peaceful man, who avoids turmoil, pays his taxes on time, and leads a boring existence. The rear is occupied by the Futurists, who are patriotic, successful, and certainly far from boring. As the last airplane reminds us, they continue to be interested in the question of Trogir.

Tullio Crali

Tullio Crali was a talented artist who resided in the town of Gorizia, near the Slovenian border. Although he exhibited his paintings all over Italy, he concentrated on Padua, Venice, and Trieste in particular. In 1940, Crali was honored with a one-man show at the Venice Biennial. Marinetti found his aeropaintings so impressive that he lectured about them on the radio.[11] In addition, he published an illustrated booklet with excerpts from numerous reviews. "The airplane [is a] natural creature," Crali declared in the preface, "which incorporates the mystery of 'cosmic motion.' It draws us inexorably upward, higher and higher every day, so we may experience God's purity more intimately and more forcefully."[12]

The booklet concluded with two aeropoems by Crali that were also conceived as visual poems. Dated 1938, the first was entitled "Altalenando sulle isole dalmate" ("Flying Back and Forth over the Dalmatian Islands").[13]

miserable dalmatians
restless wind above the islands
into the wind boreal blast
ô northwind
flying back and forth high above
grossa *lunga*
lesina *incoronata*
meleda *solta* *curzola*
WITH UNDERSEA WEBS CONCEALING INDIFFERENT
VENETIAN BANNERS THE SALTY FISHING BOATS FULL OF
SACKS AND BARRELS UNLOAD ROPES AND TAR TO CAULK
THE OLD SAILORS' AND THE OLD DISTRICTS' WRINKLES

AS OBLIVIOUS AS A WATERMELON *lissa* BOBS BLISSFULLY IN THE WATER
THE COASTAL MOUNTAINS GUARD THE HORIZON WITH CLENCHED FISTS

In contrast to Ignazio Scurto, who concentrated on a single Dalmatian island, Crali painted an aerial portrait of a number of islands. Since he was born and raised in Dalmatia (now Croatia), he knew the region well. The composition itself is divided into six different scenes, some of which are depicted visually and some of which are not. The first thing the reader learns about the coast is that the people who live there are unhappy. Although Crali does not pause to elaborate, the inhabitants are presumably dissatisfied because they are subject to Dalmatian rule. They are eager for the Italians to reclaim their former empire. Paralleling the situation on the ground, the wind turns out to be "malcontento" as well. Crali's initial remarks are surrounded by a series of curved lines representing the restless wind. Since "atalenando" means "swinging to and fro," the title suggests that Crali's airplane is being buffeted around quite a bit. While the view from the air is impressive, the experience is more chaotic than in Scurto's poem. Since the composition contains lots of local color, we can situate it precisely both in space and in time. The *bora* is a violent, cold, dry wind associated with the northern Adriatic. Blow-

17. Tullio Crali, "Altalenando sulle isole dalmate"

ing from a northerly or a northeasterly direction, its appearance signals the arrival of winter. The *tramontana* is a cold north wind coming from across the mountains, in this case the Alps. Unfortunately, Crali seems to be experiencing both of them at the same time.

Below the drawing of the wind, a string of words represents Crali's airplane flying through the air: "altalenando in quota su." Following a sudden shift in perspective, we glimpse some of the 1,185 islands that adorn the Dalmatian coast, and part of the coast itself. The section depicted in the composition extends approximately two hundred miles from Zadar, where Crali once lived, to the walled city of Dubrovnik. Since the islands all bear Serbo-Croatian names today, they are difficult to identify. As the title proclaims, Crali zigzags back and forth between them. In order to retrace his itinerary, one must read from top to bottom and from left to right. Beginning with Dugi Otok (Grossa), the northernmost island, Crali flies all the way to Mijet (Lunga), situated at the southernmost end. From there he heads up the coast to Hvar (Lesina), Šolta, and Dugi Otok (Lunga) in that order. In order to preserve normal reading conventions, he places Hvar above Šolta. In reality, however, Šolta is situated further up the coast than Hvar. Reversing direction one more time, Crali flies south to Kornat (Incoronata) and further south to Korčula (Curzola), located just above Mijet. Crali zooms in on several small fishing boats at this point that are busily unloading rope and tar. Like the *bora* and the *tramontana* encountered previously, *bragozzi* are found exclusively in the Adriatic. The *trame sottomarine* are clearly fishing nets, which have been hung up to dry. The fact that they are draped over the boats' Venetian flags may or may not be significant. Zooming back out, Crali briefly glimpses the island of Vis (Lissa), which resembles a watermelon floating in the water. Pausing to admire the coastal mountains at the end of his journey, he compares them to a silent band of sentinels.

The second poem by Crali describes flying over another group of islands, situated not in the Adriatic but in the Aegean Sea. Dated 1939, it is entitled "Sorvolando le Cicladi" ("Flying over the Cyclades").

> vento annoiato caricare a lunghe ondate il caldo umidore del Levante
> appiccicoso spalmato su strati di mica sospesa
>
> s o r v o l a r e
>
> altalendando a 2000 metri sul mare
>
> **CLA**
>
> le **CI** **DI**
>
> di vetro cemento
>
> al centro degli orizzonti sazi a nausea di azzurrini e madreperle
> riverbereanti aspri grigiori pietra nuda al sole
> ingonnelliamoci di spuma salsa tra roccia e roccia merlettando la verde
> scura bottiglia del fondo sciacquare viscidumi – alghe – miele sul
> viso collo mani

RECLAMATE PIOGGE TORRENZIALI O FRESCHI LIQUIDI SPECCHI ALPINI
nella baia al riparo contesta disputare complicando intrigui nuvolosi sui bordi in roccia aggrappati strappati dalla brezza . . . .
« . . . . non c'è tempo da perdere bisogna investire al più presto gli eserciti di arsura che invadono l'Anatolia»
ovatta a brandelli sul promontorio ferito in costa da nevrastenico pescespada
HRRRRRR HRRRRRRRRRRR HR MR HRRRR HRRRRRRRRR NO no è il motore di sinistra che annaspa e perde colpi condutture benzina filtri in battibecco scioperare cocciuti un colpo alla manetta riporta il rombo in cadenza precisa
ROOOmbare ROON ROON RON RON RON RON RON
mareggiate di suoni marmorei con zucchero cannellato sull'E G E O in siesta:
gradite isole di lucum **ZEA**
SIRA
PARO
NIO
amare di mandorla spoglie di fiori

[bored wind filling the East's hot humidor in long sticky waves spread on layers of suspended mica / f l y i n g o v e r / flying back and forth at 2,000 meters above the sea / the / **CY** / **CLA** / **DES** / of glass cement / surrounded by horizons stuffed to the point of nausea with pale blues and mother-of-pearl tones reflecting harsh grays bare stone in the sun / let's put on a skirt of the salty foam between the rocks trimming the dark bottle-green bottom with lace rinsing off slime – seaweed – honey on our face neck hands / ASK FOR TORRENTIAL RAINS OR COOL LIQUIDS ALPINE MIRRORS / in the sheltered bay contesting disputing complicating cloudy intrigues on the rocky edges grasped tugged by the breeze . . . . / ". . . . . don't forget we need to assemble a mighty army as quickly as possible in order to invade Anatolia" / tufts of cotton on the headland wounded in the side by an irritable swordfish / **HRRRRRR HRRRRRRRRRRR HR MR HRRRR HRRRRRRRRR NO no the left engine is coughing and sputtering gas lines gasoline squabbling filters stubbornly going on strike an adjustment to the throttle restores the engine's precise rhythm ROOOaring ROAR ROAR RO RO RO RO RO** / swells of marble sounds with cinnamon sugar on the sleepy A E G E A N: / congenial islands of lokum / **KEA** / **SYROS** / **PAROS** / **IOS** / loved by almonds / clothed in flowers]

In contrast to the preceding poem, which was situated in winter, "Sorvolando le Cicladi" takes place during the dog days of summer. Whereas the wind in the Adriatic consisted of sharp, icy blasts, the Aegean wind is hot, lazy, and bored. Although there is a slight breeze, it is not enough to alleviate the oppressive heat and humidity. Since the climate is normally hot and dry, a new front must be passing through the area. Whatever the explanation, it produces a curious atmospheric effect in the eastern Mediterranean, where the clouds are spread out like jam on a slice of toast. Crali compares them to layers of mica, which suggests they are long, flat, and thin. In general, the composition's visual effects are fairly rudimentary. In addition to three visual analogies, it contains several elementary typographical effects. At the upper right, the word "sorvolare" represents the poet's airplane, which has leveled off at 2,000 meters and is flying in a straight line. Crali inserts a space between each of the letters in order to make the word longer. Directly below, the notation **CI / CLA / DI** represents the three northernmost islands, which form a semi-circle like the syllables on the page. Viewed from an airplane, the sea seems to be made of glass and the islands of cement. Looking all around him, the poet complains that the horizon is drenched in pale iridescent hues, which he finds nauseating. "Pietra nuda al sole" may refer to one of the islands baking in the sun or simply to a large rock. Among other things, the phrase reminds us that the Cyclades are arid and the soil is thin. Since rain is a precious commodity, Crali parodies an advertising campaign a few lines later, demanding that readers ask for torrential downpours.

Beginning with a playful neologism ("ingonnelliamoci," literally "let's skirtify ourselves"), the next section presents a number of problems. Gathering up the delicate foam from the shoreline, the poet exhorts his companions to join him in making skirts for themselves trimmed with seaweed. —Or does he? As one quickly perceives, too many things are wrong with this interpretation. How can Crali be on the ground if he is flying an airplane? Where did his companions come from? And when did he start wearing women's clothing? The explanation seems to be that the scene is purely fictitious. Zooming in on an imaginary setting, Crali pictures a family enjoying themselves at the seashore. The (awkward) use of ellipses in this section suggests the words in question are spoken by one of the imaginary characters. They should have quotation marks around them, as in a later sentence. In all probability the speaker is a young girl who, spying the beautiful foam, urges her friends to decorate themselves with it. When they grow tired of the game, they simply rinse the foam off. While the children are playing in the water, the adults sunbathe (or sit in the shade) and talk among themselves. Inspired perhaps by Germany's invasion of Czechoslovakia on March 15, one of the men insists that Greece should invade Turkey. The last sentence, which is purely descriptive, presents a special challenge. One suspects the tufts of cotton are really trees and that the angry swordfish is an old-fashioned sailing vessel moored at a dock.

Crali's reverie is interrupted at this point by a sudden emergency that requires all of his attention. One of the airplane's engines is threatening to quit. Fortunately, after a moment of suspense, the problem proves easy to correct. Adjusting the throttle, he increases the flow of gas and averts a potentially dangerous situation. The poem concludes with a final glimpse of the islands dozing in the sun. From the air, the poet jokes, the whitewashed houses look like pieces of Greek candy covered with powdered sugar. Since the Cyclades are far too numerous to depict visually, Crali chooses four representative islands. Kea (Zea) possesses important temple ruins and a picturesque monastery. Syros (Sira) contains the largest town in the Cyclades and the oldest acropolis. Paros (Paro) was the site of a famous marble quarry in antiquity. And Ios (Nio) is supposedly where Homer is buried. With one exception, the position of the islands on the page corresponds to their geographical positions in the Aegean. In actuality, Ios is located to the southeast of Paros. Although the Cyclades are hot and dry in the summer, Crali seems to say, they are covered with almond blossoms and countless flowers in the spring.

6
Brazilian Concrete Poetry

In 1952, three poets formed a group in São Paulo, Brazil, that was destined to become extremely influential: Augusto de Campos, his brother Haroldo de Campos, and Décio Pignatari. Paralleling a similar but independent development in Europe, the Noigandres group, as they came to be known, sought to exploit the physical properties of language.[1] Determined to revolutionize modern poetry, they began to experiment with the placement of words on the page, their sound, their physical appearance, and their interrelation to one another. Before long—the chronology is complicated—both groups began to refer to their creations as "Concrete" poetry.[2] Like their European counterparts, the Brazilians treated words as visual and phonetic counters to be manipulated without regard to their meaning. "The concrete poem is an object in and of itself," they proclaimed, "not an interpreter of external objects and/or sensations that are more or less subjective."[3] Whereas traditional poetry operates on the conceptual level, Concrete poetry is based on perception. It differs from conventional verse in its ability to translate abstract ideas into visual images. This ability is what makes it concrete. In the absence of conventional grammar, Concrete poetry employs a spatial syntax. Words are free to combine with each other visually as well as verbally, vertically as well as horizontally.

Augusto de Campos

During the first half of 1953, Augusto de Campos wrote a series of poems that embodied this brand-new aesthetic. Entitled *Poetamenos* (*Poetminus*), the volume was inspired by Anton Webern's *Klangfarbenmelodie* (*Color Tone Poems*) and Ezra Pound's *Cantos*.[4] The poems were intended not only to be read in the traditional manner but also to be recited by multiple voices.[5] In order to indicate which parts were reserved for which speakers, de Campos color-coded the words (and certain syllables).

Some of the works were designed for two voices, others for as many as five. Despite the obvious interest of such a procedure, production costs forced the poet to abandon his initial program. His current Website suggests he would have published all his poetry in color if he could have. For better or worse, black and white proved to be an excellent vehicle for the Noigandres poets because it allowed them to focus on structural concerns. "Concrete poetry begins by becoming aware of graphic space as structural agent," the trio announced in 1958; "The concrete poem communicates its own structure."[6] Published two years earlier, the following text is the first part of a longer poem composed of four circular compositions.

o v o
n o v e l o
novo no velho
o filho em folhos
na jaula dos joelhos
infante em fonte
f e t o f e i t o
d e n t r o d o
centro[7]

[egg / ball of yarn / new not old / the son in ruffles / in the cage of the knees / infant in source / fetus made / inside the / center].

Although the text's visual appearance is attractive, even seductive, it is highly atypical—at least for the three poets examined in this chapter. According to the theory they presented in the Pilot Plan for Concrete Poetry in 1958, it illustrates the first stage in the evolution of Concrete poetry, which is based on physical resemblance. In addition to evoking the egg verbally, the composition also depicts the egg visually. Interestingly, de Campos condemned Apollinaire for succumbing to the same pictographic temptation in an article published the very same year.[8] As practiced by the Noigandres group, Concrete poetry was, and continues to be, fiercely antimimetic. In keeping with the project outlined in the Pilot Plan, the vast majority of the compositions are dynamic and nonrepresentational.[9]

The present text celebrates the incredible potential of the human egg, which miraculously develops into a fetus and eventually into a baby. The egg's circular shape is reflected not only by the visual design but also by two additional objects: the ball of yarn and the uterus in which the fetus is growing. According to de Campos, the womb is not only the source but also the center of humanity, since ultimately everything revolves about it. Discussing a similar work, which will be examined later, he provides the following gloss for **novelo**: "implying the complication of the human being."[10] This appears to refer to biological complication rather than to the complications inherent in human existence. Thus the relationship between the first two words would seem to be metaphoric. Like a ball of yarn, which reveals innumerable twists and turns as it unrolls, the egg divides and redivides innumerable times to produce the complicated animal we call homo sapiens. The poet envisions the young child dressed in ruffles and playing beneath his or her parents' knees.

As de Campos declares, eggs are associated with things that are new, not with things that have grown old. They are associated with birth rather than with death. In fact, this construction holds the key to much of the poem—not at the semantic but at the phonemic level. The text incorporates two acoustical structures that reflect, illustrate, and embody two important themes. Each structure complements the other but also competes with it. The first theme is that of birth and rebirth, which is evoked by the metamorphosis that continually takes place in the poem. The syllables in the first two lines are rearranged, for example, to form the third line. **Filho** is transformed into **folho**, **jaula** into **joelho**, **infante** into **em fonte**, and so forth. Viewed from a different angle, a second theme emerges which, for lack of a better term, might be called "security." According to the printed text, the first expression is not transformed into the second but is simply juxtaposed with it. Five pairs of words are placed in opposition to each other to form a protective shell (or membrane). The egg is in the center, shielded by the acoustic walls that surround it.

Augusto de Campos published a poem entitled "**uma vez**" the following year that is more representative of his early work. Like most of his poetry, it is concentrated, abstract, and dynamic.

uma vez
uma fala
uma foz
uma vez uma bala
uma fala uma voz
uma foz uma vala
uma bala uma vez
uma voz
uma vala
uma vez

> [one time / one speech / one river mouth / one time / one bullet / one speech / one voice / one river mouth / one ditch / one bullet / one time / one voice / one ditch / one time].

Like the preceding text, "**uma vez**" illustrates James Joyce's concept of the verbivocovisual, which was enthusiastically adopted by the Noigandres group. The poem is composed of words, it appeals to the eye, and it is designed to be read aloud. Indeed, Claus Clüver reports that a recording exists of the text featuring two male voices and two female voices.[11] At first glance, the composition resembles a capital Z that has been tilted on its side. The two transverse strokes and the two diagonal strokes are exactly the same length. Each contains four pairs of words that echo each other in a complicated ballet. Eventually, however, one perceives that the design is composed of two acute angles facing in opposite directions, which changes its whole Gestalt. The main problem that occurs is how to determine the correct reading order—assuming that such a thing exists. Depending on whether one follows literary conventions or artistic conventions, there would seem to be two possible paths. One can read from left to right and from top to bottom, as I have done in my translation, or one can decipher the figure on the right followed by the figure on the left. The second model produces the following poem: "one time / one speech / one river mouth / one bullet / one voice / one ditch / one time / one time / one speech / one river mouth / one bullet / one voice / one ditch."

Both of these reading strategies generate interesting rhyme schemes. The literary model begins ABCA, adds three symmetrical couplets BBCCBB, and reverses the first four lines ACBA. The artistic model begins ABCB, reverses the first three lines CBA, and repeats the whole process. Visually, the two figures mirror each other, but acoustically they are identical. Since B (**fala** / **bala** / **vala**) concludes every other line, it provides a pleasant rhyming constant. The question remains: which of these two strategies is correct? Interestingly, the recording described by Clüver follows both models. The first reading proceeds along the diagonals, while the second scans the poem horizontally. Beginning with "**uma bala**" on the left, the recital concludes with yet another reading. The four voices advance along the two diagonals simultaneously to create an example of Concrete polyphony. Instead of attempting to privilege a single reading, the conductor fashions an acoustic tapestry composed of multiple readings. Since de Campos's own recordings observe a similar strategy, this seems to be the wisest approach. Instead of one poem, the composition contains many poems. Or to put it another way, the composition consists of all possible readings.

No matter which path the reader ultimately chooses, some sort of drama appears to be taking place. Or rather, since "**uma vez**" can also be translated as "once upon a time," the poem appears to recount an event that happened in the past. Since there are no verbs to link the six nouns together, the relations between them must be intuited. Although the plot remains the same no matter how one proceeds, some versions of the story are more satisfying than others. The artistic reading model is probably the most rewarding because it is concise, linear, and to the point. From what the reader can gather, someone was giving a speech by the mouth of a river when he was shot and killed. He barely had time to cry out before he fell dead. And he was buried in a ditch. The numerical logic is inexorable: one man was killed by one bullet and buried in one ditch. It could scarcely be otherwise. Who this individual was, what he was speaking about, and why he was killed are never made clear. Was it a political assassination? A crime of passion? A case of mistaken identity? An unfortunate accident? For better or worse, we will never know.

Concrete poetry requires "the dynamic utilization of typographical resources," Augusto de Campos explained in 1956, because their normal arrangement is "incapable of serving the whole range of inflections of which poetic thought is capable."[12] As the next poem demonstrates, there is no need to resort to extravagant typographical effects to accomplish this goal. Amazing results can be achieved simply by using italics or boldface letters. Concrete poetry has been committed to a minimalist aesthetic from the very beginning. Paradoxically, as Rudolf Arnheim observes, "it achieves an expansion of possible readings by a reduction of means."[13] Among other things, this operation is evident in the choice of the composition's typeface. Like so many Concrete poems, it is printed in lower case letters, which are then enlarged to form a kind of poster poem.

c o l o c a r a m a s
c a r a c o l o c a r
a m a s **c a r a c o l**
o c a r a m a s **c a r**
a c o l o c a r a m a
s **c a r a c o l** o c a
r a m a s **c a r a c o**
l o c a r a m a s **c a**
r a c o l o c a r a m
a s **c a r a c o l** o c
a r a m a s **c a r a c**
o l o c a r a m a s **c**
a r a c o l o c a r a
m a s **c a r a c o l** o
c a r a m a s **c a r a**

Composed in 1960, this ingenious little poem was generated by repeating a single expression over and over: "colocar a mascara" ("to put on a mask"). By eliminating the break between the last word of one phrase and the first word of the next, de Campos generates a second word as well, which he prints in boldface letters: "**caracol**" ("**snail**"). Since the basic expression has fifteen letters, but the distance between the left and right margins is only eleven letters, the poet is continually forced to wrap it around. A phrase that is cut off at the end of one line simply continues on the next line, observing the poem's virtual boundaries while preserving its linguistic integrity. Like the snail itself, the word for snail descends the invisible pillar line by line until it reaches the bottom. As much as anything, the beauty of this procedure stems from its enormous simplicity. In addition, it illustrates the Noigandres group's conviction, repeated again and again, that Concrete poetry should be analogical and isomorphic. The form of a poem should ideally reflect the poem's subject without imitating its physical appearance. "At a more advanced state," the Pilot Plan proclaims, "isomorphism tends to resolve itself into pure structural movement."[14] This describes the work reproduced above.

Now that we understand how the poem operates, how are we to understand the poem itself? Is it simply an amusing portrait of a snail descending a post? The fact that the mollusk is surrounded by disguises, the fact that it participates in these disguises (at least linguistically), suggests otherwise. But what kind of relationship exists between these two entities? The poet's brother, Haroldo de Campos, provides a masterful interpretation: the composition represents "the masking and unmasking of the poem's process. Like a snail slowly unfolding its going."[15] Like the tardy mollusk wending its way toward its destination, the poet gradually writes the work, and the reader gradually deciphers it. The above composition not only describes this double procedure but also reenacts it at the same time. The missing link between the snail and the mask turns out to be the words of which the poem is composed. If the material of Concrete poetry is generally language, as Mary Ellen Solt affirms, the same observation applies to its subject matter.[16] Concrete poetry is obsessed with the spoken and the written word.

The final poem by Augusto de Campos, which recalls the first composition we examined, was published two years later. As Haroldo de Campos remarks, it is "another generative poem, this time with cosmic and existential hints. A kind of 'portable cosmogony' in cross-word form."[17]

```
      o
  n o v e l o
  o v o
o v o             s o l
  e               o
  l               l e t r a
  o               e
              e s t r e l a     t
              s   r             e
      s o l e t r a             r
      o   e   r                 r
      l   t   e                 e
          r   l             t e m o r
          a   a                 o
                        t       t     t
                        e     m o r t e
              t e r r e m o t o       r
                        o     r       m e t r o
                        r     t       o
                            t e r m o     m   m
                                  e         m o t o r
                                  t       m o t o r
                                  r         t o r t o
                                  o       m o r t o
                                            r   o
```

[ball of yarn / egg / egg / ball of yarn / egg / egg // sun / letter / star / spells out / sun / letter / star / spells out // fear / death / earthquake / meter / term / fear / death / earthquake / meter / term // motive / motive / unjust / death / motive / motive / unjust / death]

One thing is clear at first glance: the composition represents a stunning achievement. Not only is its interlocking design a marvel of geometric precision, but the figures that compose it are endowed with a crystalline purity. Adding to the poem's visual appeal, the version that appears in Solt's anthology is printed in white letters on a solid blue background. While in theory, the reader could begin anywhere, the fact that the poem descends from the upper left to the lower right suggests that this is the preferred sequence. As in conventional poetry, one reads from left to right and from top to bottom. Like "**uma vez**," each figure contains two identical groups of words. The vertical words echo the horizontal words and vice versa. The most productive strategy, which I have followed in my translation, seems to be to read the horizontal lines first and then the vertical lines. The whole composition is structured like a symphony with four distinct movements. In the same manner as the first two lines of "**ovo novelo**," the initial figure celebrates the mystery of life. Like the ball of yarn, whose shape and complexity it shares, the egg possesses enormous potential. Just as the yarn is eventually transformed into a sweater, the egg gradually evolves into a complex animal.

The second figure celebrates the mystery of the universe, which, like Nature in Baudelaire's "Correspondances," occasionally emits confused (and confusing) words. Whereas the words in Baudelaire's poem are whispered to passersby, those in the present composition possess a visual form. Composed of heavenly bodies like the sun and the stars, they form a celestial text that has to be spelled out letter by letter. And yet, simple as it sounds, the process is fraught with anxiety. Some of the words lack letters, some are illegible, and others are missing altogether. Inevitably, despite a few tantalizing glimpses, the heavenly message eludes the viewer. By contrast, the third figure evokes life on earth, which leaves a great deal to be desired. According to de Campos, human existence is dominated by fear and death—in that order. Much of daily life is threatening, and no matter how hard one struggles, it inevitably ends with his or her demise. Rather than an idyllic haven, the planet is a dangerous place to live, where earthquakes can swallow one up without warning. The fact that "**termo**" can be combined with "**metro**" to form the Portuguese word for "thermometer" reminds us that humanity is subject to numerous diseases as well. Confronted with life's absurdities, the fourth figure is anything but comforting. Since "motor" is both a noun and an adjective, it may refer to the "engine" that drives the absurd universe or, as I suspect, to the Supreme Being's "motive" for constructing that universe. Whatever the explanation, death is depicted as wrong, unjust, and unfair (all meanings of "torto"). What kind of Creator would invent a machine that self-destructs?

Looking back over the composition, one notes that it covers the entire gamut of human existence, from the moment of conception to the moment of death. In addition to the work's existential preoccupations, it possesses a cosmic dimension that prompts Solt to call it "an object of shining spiritual quality."[18] The arrangement of the words on the page mirrors that of the stars in the heavens, and vice versa. In actuality the poem is concerned with two constellations, one poetic and the other celestial, one visible and the other merely imagined. Like the poem, the universe is composed of intelligible signs that demand to be deciphered. In several respects, the composition recalls Mallarmé's *Un Coup de dés jamais n'abolira le hasard* (*A Throw of the Dice Will Never Abolish Chance*), which is spread across the page like "UNE CONSTELLATION froide d'oubli" (A CONSTELLATION cold with oblivion") and which must also be deciphered word by word. As Augusto de Campos declares, Mallarmé's revolutionary poem "[opened] the door on a new poetic reality."[19]

Haroldo de Campos

Haroldo de Campos was a prolific translator and literary critic as well as an accomplished poet. "Guided by theory and research," K. David Jackson notes, "Haroldo's poly-faceted production across genres includes poetry, theory, translation, criticism, the essay, conferences, interviews, and university courses."[20] Throughout his work, K. Alfons Knauth adds, "there is a constant concern with the materiality of language, with verbal world making and the processing of a Concrete, multilingual literature."[21] This preoccupation may be seen in his Concrete poetry in particular, where the linguistic sign's semantic function is eclipsed by material concerns. In poem after poem, signification is sacrificed to visual and acoustic requirements. In Concrete poetry in general, Solt explains, "form = content and content = form."[22] What you see—and what you hear—is basically what you get. This is especially true of Haroldo de Campos's most advanced poetry, in which, to quote the Pilot Plan, "isomorphism tends to resolve itself into pure structural movement . . . ; geometrical form and the mathematics of composition prevail."[23] Published in 1957, the first poem demonstrates what the document means.

<table>
<tr><td>branco</td><td>branco</td><td>branco</td><td>branco</td></tr>
<tr><td>vermelho</td><td></td><td></td><td></td></tr>
<tr><td>estanco</td><td>vermelho</td><td></td><td></td></tr>
<tr><td></td><td>espelho</td><td>vermelho</td><td></td></tr>
<tr><td></td><td></td><td>estanco</td><td>branco[24]</td></tr>
</table>

[white white white white / red / I stanch red / (I) mirror red / I stanch white]

In contrast to the poetry examined in the previous section, this composition is largely abstract. Consisting of four apparently unrelated words scattered across the page, it is totally devoid of conventional content. The most that can be said is that two of the words refer to colors. The other two denote an object and an action that, in the absence of an interpretive context, are deprived of any significance. Or conceivably, since **espelho** means both "mirror" and "I mirror," they denote two actions. As Philadelpho Menezes observes, "Concrete poetry's novelty in terms of compositional procedure is its installation of a new syntax based on relations of similarity among words: parataxis."[25] Words are juxtaposed with each other solely according to their physical properties. What holds them together is place they occupy, and the role they play, in the poem's total gestalt. Conceived as a visual shape, Claus Clüver comments, "the whole text . . . asks to be perceived instantaneously and simultaneously."[26] Deciphering its verbal message, on the other hand, is considerably more complicated—not because it is difficult to grasp but because there are several competing paths. Indeed, Clüver reports that a musical score exists that explores multiple horizontal, vertical, and diagonal possibilities.[27]

Although it is tempting to conclude that the words may be read in virtually any order, this conclusion is almost certainly mistaken. Reading from left to right and from top to bottom, for example, produces the uninspired translation given above. Reversing this procedure, on the other hand, generates the following sequence: "white / red / I stanch / white / red / (I) mirror / white / red / I stanch / white / white." While the words are only counters, their relationship to each other is clear, even in English translation. The poem consists of three parallel statements (each composed of three words and ending with a verb in the first person) and concludes, like the Shakespearean sonnet, with a final couplet. Red alternates with white in a cyclical dance, until white triumphs at the end. To be sure, it sounds much better in Portuguese: "**branco / vermelho / estanco / branco / vermelho / espelho / branco / vermelho / estanco / branco / branco**." De Campos himself provides the following commentary: "A progression with the word *branco* (white). In counterpoint, the word *vermelho* (red). The internal rhymes provide the skeleton. . . . The maximum opening of the poem coincides with the maximum blank of the page: a coinformation, at visual level, with the effect of white color over a white surface in painting, or the word white written with white ink on white paper."[28]

The reading strategy described above is not only the most rewarding approach but also, as far as can be ascertained, the one adopted by the poet himself. The poem is divided into four vertical columns, each of which begins with the word "**branco**." As the reader deciphers each of the columns, the word progresses from left to right—not all at once, as with a horizontal reading, but in carefully measured steps, each of which is punctuated by the word "**vermelho**." As the reader continues, the visual gap between "**branco**" and "**vermelho**" becomes wider and wider until, at the end, the latter has completely disappeared. At this point, as de Campos declares, the verbal and the visual progressions come to essentially the same conclusion. The white space is framed at the top and bottom by the word for "white," and the word for "white" at the top and bottom is illustrated by the white space. In addition, the theme of white-on-white recalls several poems by Mallarmé that employ an identical color scheme.

Although the previous poem is largely nonrepresentational, it contains occasional references to recognizable objects and actions. By contrast, the next poem is completely abstract. Composed of conjunctions, prepositions, and comparative adjectives, it refers to such concepts as size, quantity, and intensity.

mais	**mais**							
menos	**mais**	**e**	**menos**					
	mais	**ou**	**menos**	**sem**	**mais**			
				nem	**menos**	**nem**	**mais**	
						nem	**menos**	**menos**

[more more / less more and less / more or less without more / neither less nor more / nor less less]

Since "**mais**" can also be translated as "**plus**" and "**menos**" as "**minus,**" several critics have suggested that the poem represents a mathematical equation. Viewed in this perspective, the reader would presumably need to solve the equation in order to arrive at the poem's final meaning. While the presence of five conjunctions and a troublesome preposition complicates this task, the composition appears to be divided into two symmetrical halves separated by the word "**ou.**" Since "**mais**" and "**menos**" oscillate back and forth between two meanings, the first half might also be translated as "more + more / – more and – / more." If we treat this as an equation, the four terms add up to zero (2a – 2a = 0). Unfortunately, it does not seem possible to extract a meaningful solution from the second half, which is much more ambiguous. Although one can make similar substitutions, none of the results are significant. Perhaps the solution we are seeking is actually much simpler. While "**mais**" occurs four times in the first half and "**menos**" twice, for example, the proportions are reversed in the second half. Perhaps the positive and the negative charges simply cancel each other out, as they presumably do in the universe in general.

Or perhaps the explanation has nothing to do with mathematics after all. Upon reflection, one perceives that the poem illustrates the Zen Buddhist philosophy that "less is more." Or rather, since it begins with "**mais**" and concludes with "**menos,**" it expresses the conviction that "more is less." The first two words serve as a prelude and the last two words as a coda. The transformation from the first concept to the second occurs in the space of three short lines. **Mais** and **menos** alternate with each other until it has been completed. Taking place right before our eyes, the conversion demonstrates the truth of the very principle it espouses. As we have seen, Concrete poetry shares the same minimalist philosophy. By the judicious rendering of a few choice words, it manages to transform less into more. The fascination it exerts on the reader, the viewer, and the listener stems from the contrast between its limited means and its disproportionate effect.

Compared to the previous two poems, which employ highly restricted vocabularies, the following composition is positively verbose. Whereas the first work is composed of four words and the other work (for all practical purposes) of two, "**fala prata**" utilizes eight different terms. With two noteworthy exceptions, each word is repeated at least twice.

fala
prata

cala
ouro

cara
prata

coroa
ouro

fala
cala

para

prata ouro
cala fala

clara

[speech / silver / silence / gold / heads / silver / tails / gold / speech / silence / halt / silver / silence / gold / speech / clarity]

This time Haroldo de Campos sets out to deconstruct a well-known proverb: "Speech is silver, silence is golden." Formulated for the first time around 600 AD, in the Judaic biblical commentaries called the *Midrash*, the expression serves as the poem's point of departure.[29] The first pair of words, "**fala / prata**," reminds us that a gifted speaker is known as "a silver-tongued orator." He not only possesses a valuable talent, but he also renders valuable advice. However, the second pair of words, "**cala / ouro**," portrays the subject in a different light. Speech may well be precious, as traditional wisdom maintains, but silence is even more precious. Since the two can scarcely coexist at the same time, the second statement effectively contradicts the first statement. To somebody who is engaged in silent meditation, speech is obviously unwelcome. By the same token, however, to somebody who is waiting for a reply to a question, silence is equally unwelcome. If silence is priceless, speech must be worthless, and if speech is priceless, silence must be worthless. How can we reconcile the two statements? The remainder of the poem explores this rhetorical paradox and attempts to find a satisfactory solution.

The next two pairs of words, like the first two, are obviously juxtaposed with each other. This time, gold and silver are associated with the opposite sides of a coin. Since coins were once made of precious metals, this makes a certain amount of sense. Nevertheless, the relationship between the two turns out to be metaphorical instead of metonymic. The next pair of words, "**fala**" / "**cala**," makes it clear that the metaphor describes the problem introduced at the beginning of the poem. Deciding whether silence is more valuable than speech or vice versa is like flipping a coin. Sometimes heads comes up, and sometimes tails. At this point, two reading strategies present themselves, one primarily visual and the other literary. Readers can continue to the end of the diagonal, or they can continue to read from top to bottom and from left to right. On the one hand, the fact that the poem consists of pairs of words suggests that "**clara**" should be followed by "**para**." On the other hand, the literary path makes more sense from a structural point of view. "**Para**" would interrupt the poem's binary rhythm and prepare the reader for the double conclusion: "**prata**" / "**cala**" and "**ouro**" / "**fala**." Stressing the conclusion's clarity, "**clara**" would serve as an epigram.

The composition concludes, in either case, with two images whose presence is extremely ironic: silver silence and golden speech. Although this development is a logical outgrowth of the preceding discussion, it catches the reader entirely by surprise. Unexpectedly, each cliché has been transformed into its structural opposite. The original proverb has been revised to read "silence is silver, speech is golden." The lesson illustrated by this reversal is perfectly clear: whether speech or silence is more valuable varies according to the context. In the absence of absolute values, the decision is a toss-up.[30] Like the preceding poem, moreover, the composition conceals an aesthetic program disguised as a philosophical statement. Since the acoustic element in Brazilian Concrete poetry is as important as the visual element, neither one is more valuable than the other. Sound and image not only complement each other but coexist in perfect harmony. Readers may choose either to contemplate a Concrete poem or to recite it out loud (or both). Sometimes silence is more profitable than speech, and sometimes it is not.

Frequently anthologized, the final poem by Haroldo de Campos is probably his best-known composition. Not only is it more accessible than much of his poetry, but its subject is also immediately recognizable.

cristal
cristal
fome
cristal
cristal
fome de forma
cristal
cristal
forma de fome
cristal
cristal
forma

[crystal / crystal / hunger / crystal / crystal / hunger for form / crystal / crystal / form of hunger / crystal / crystal / form]

Like the previous works, the composition illustrates the poet's conviction that, at least in art, less is more. Utilizing only three nouns and a preposition, it celebrates the crucial role of form in aesthetic creation. Although the poem is concerned with the concept in general, the visual design evokes geometric form. More precisely, it evokes the symmetrical structures associated with gems and minerals. As soon as one begins to decipher the poem, it becomes necessary to choose between two separate reading strategies. Illustrated by the above translation, the literary model requires the reader to proceed from left to right and from top to bottom. The artistic model offers an equally rewarding path. Since the visual design is divided into three parts, readers may proceed section by section instead. Consisting of the word "**crystal**" repeated four times, the two outer sections are practically identical. Although each figure is perfectly symmetrical, they are mirror images of each other. A similar symmetrical reversal governs the middle section, whose two halves also mirror each other. Thus the poem possesses the same crystalline structure that it seeks to glorify. Each of the outer sections comprises a simple cubic lattice, like that of table salt. While only four edges are visible, they allow us to reconstruct its familiar outline. Because the middle section has vertical protrusions, it is more difficult to identify. Extensive research suggests it resembles certain crystals that possess a "high-pressure *Te* structure."[31]

As the central section implies, human beings have an aesthetic appetite that differentiates them from all other animals. Although they thirst for knowledge, they also hunger for some kind of form in their lives. Nevertheless, the phrases in question do not refer to the human condition so much as to the condition of art. More precisely, they allude to the demands that the aesthetic object places on the artist. Like a crystal, an artistic creation can be viewed as a potential structure, as a series of empty spaces reserved for the appropriate "atom." As long as it waits for the artist to add the right touch, it can be said to have a hunger for form. Since it is a virtual structure, however, it can only exhibit that hunger in the form of hunger that has been fulfilled, i.e., as a finished art object. Thus the latter represents both the hunger for form and the form which that hunger assumes. Without form, the poem seems to say, art is not really possible. Beauty, like meaning, cannot exist without some kind of structure.

Décio Pignatari

The third member of the Noigandres group, Décio Pignatari, taught industrial design and communication theory for many years. In addition, he composed the most famous Concrete poem in Brazil, "beba coca cola," which compares the American soft drink to a series of nauseating substances. Since several critics have analyzed this poem, it has been omitted from the present chapter. Together with Luiz Ángelo Pinto, Pignatari also invented "semiotic poetry," which employs visual signs instead of words. However, it is his experiments with Concrete poetry that interest us here. Dating from 1956, the following poem is arranged to form a spiral rotating about a vertical axis consisting of a series of "m"s.

u m
m o v i
m e n t o
c o m p o n d o
a l é m
d a
n u v e m
u m
c a m p o
d e
c o m b a t e

m i r a
g e m
i r a
d e
u m
h o r i z o n t e
p u r o
n u m
m o
m e n t o
v i v o[32]

[a / move / ment / composing / a / field / of / battle / beyond / the / cloud / mira / ge / fury / of / a / pure / horizon / at a / vivid / mo / ment]

That the composition is concerned with motion is apparent from the very beginning. As Iumna Simon and Vinicius Dantas note, it presents "a kinetic representation of its own content."[33] Extending the length of the poem, from "movimento" to "momento," the vertical axis anchors the revolving words and prevents them from flying off the page. In contrast to its physical appearance, the composition's vocabulary is largely unremarkable. Similarly, despite a few phonic echoes, there is no systematic attempt at rhyming. Although the poem's language is perfectly ordinary, the finished text is unusual. At first glance, it seems to be curiously abstract. While there are a number of references to natural phenomena, for example, these appear to be juxtaposed at random. Since verbs are practically nonexistent, readers are forced to intuit the relationships between various components, several of which appear to be metaphors. In addition, as we will see in a moment, the composition possesses an extraordinary degree of ambiguity. Together with certain thematic considerations, these stylistic traits suggest that it was inspired by Mallarmé in particular.

The composition begins with a cryptic statement centered around a present participle—the only verb in the whole work. Some kind of movement is supposedly composing a battlefield. However, since motion is not endowed with agency, how it can possibly compose anything? And what in any case does it mean to compose a field of battle? Complicating the scenario still further, "além" can also mean "above," and "nuvem" can describe a "moving throng." The mysterious action could conceivably be taking place above the cloud rather than behind it, and the cloud itself could actually be a group of people. Similarly, "miragem" may not refer to a mirage at all but simply to an "illusion." Without further details, there is simply no way to tell. Despite these momentary setbacks, the second half contains an allusion that finally permits us to decipher the poem. Although many of the references are obscure, the presence of an "horizonte" and a "momento vivo" suggests we are witnessing a vivid sunset. Unexpectedly, the poem turns out to be a landscape. The question that arises at this point is: who is the artist? An anonymous painter or Pignatari himself? Once again, for better or for worse, it is impossible to say. The poem may be a description of a landscape painting or of an actual landscape. In the last analysis, it does not make a great deal of difference. In either case, since the composition is a virtual creation, the scene it depicts is an illusion. The movement evoked at the beginning is that of the artist's hand, either real or metaphorical, painting the battle scene in question. Mirroring the furious soldiers on the battlefield, the setting sun bathes the scene in a blood-red glow.

José Lino Grünewald

José Lino Grünewald was a lawyer, journalist, and well-known film critic who joined the Noigandres group in 1958. In several respects, the following composition resembles Augusto de Campos's "caracol" and Décio Pignatari's "um movimento." Like them, it is a self-reflexive poem that is both dynamic and isomorphic.

```
êsse          solo
              calo
êsse sol
              cal
êsse só
              cá
êsse s
              c(esse
```
[34]

[that soil / callus / that sun / lime / that solitary / here / that s / c(eases]

Like the two works mentioned above, "êsse solo" enacts what it depicts and depicts what it enacts. In general, auto-illustrative poetry that possesses a visual dimension utilizes one of two procedures. Either it portrays the subject in question, like Guillaume Apollinaire's calligrams, or it illustrates the principle that the subject represents, like some of the Italian Futurists' poetry. As mentioned earlier, the Brazilians rejected the first practice but embraced the second enthusiastically. Indeed, the concept of visual isomorphic form is identical to that of the Futurists' *analogia disegnata* (see chapter 2). As we have seen, a principle may be invoked in two ways. It may be associated with a particular object, like "caracol," or with an abstract category, like "um movimento." Although both poems are concerned with movement, the first one manages to evoke the animal as well, simply by naming it. Like the second work, Grünewald's composition illustrates an abstract concept: disappearance. The initial expression in each column undergoes a progressive reduction from one line to the next. The operation proceeds carefully and inexorably, deleting one letter at a time. By the end of the poem, "**solo**" and "**calo**" have been reduced to their initial letters. As the poet notes in the last line, they will cease to exist if the operation continues. At both the visual and the acoustic levels, the poem performs its own disappearing act.

While the composition is perfectly coherent visually and phonetically, the verbal message does not appear to make much sense. Although every other line begins with the word "**êsse**" which alludes to a specific antecedent, we have no idea what that antecedent might be. For better or worse, the poem exists in a referential vacuum. Several linguistic peculiarities exist as well that seem to have no justification. For instance, in the fifth line, a demonstrative adjective modifies a descriptive adjective, which is grammatically impossible. And for some unknown reason, the very last word employs the subjunctive tense rather than the indicative.

In addition, some terms have more than one meaning. "Solo" can also be translated as "by one's self," for example; "calo" as "blister," and "cal" as "whitewash." Finally, the relations between the various words that make up the composition are far from evident. Only with great effort does one succeed in constructing a provisional scenario. Without belaboring the point, the poem appears to be a Concrete version of the pastoral elegy. Mixing metonymy and metaphor, it laments the condition of the Brazilian peasantry and offers an ironic consolation. The first four lines evoke the brutal hardships of peasant life. Although the poor farmer toils endlessly in the fields, he receives little more than calluses for his pains. Burnt to a crisp by the blazing sun, which burns like quicklime, he is the very image of futility. The last four lines evoke the peasant's solitary existence on earth, ignored by Church and State alike. His only relief comes—and this is scarcely much comfort—when he ceases to exist.

The second poem paints a picture of life in general which, no matter what part of the world one inhabits, is characterized by four constants. Depending on one's point of view, the portrait is either amusing or depressing.

a v i d a
c o m i d a
a v i d a
b e b i d a
a v i d a
d o r m i d a
a v i d a
i d a

[life / food / life / drink / life / sleep / life / gone]

That the three necessities of life happen to rhyme with the past participle of "to go" is fortuitous, to say the least. Portuguese and Spanish may be the only languages in the world where this is possible. Beginning with a phonetic relationship that is merely coincidental, Grünewald constructs a poetic scenario in which each word plays a significant role. The first three words designate actions that are essential for human existence. In order to survive, human beings need to eat, drink, and sleep. The fourth word reminds us that, sooner or later, life comes to an end. For better or worse, the preceding facts describe the human condition. Since the composition contains no active verbs, it resembles a shopping list more than a traditional poem. Alternating with each of the four words in turn, the refrain "**a vida**" stresses life's fundamental importance. The fact that each line ends with the same three letters interjects a humorous note. However, since "–ida" means "gone," it evokes life's transience at the same time. That "comida," "bebida," and "dormida" are past participles emphasizes the finality of the actions in question. They imply that life has already been consumed, that it is too late to make amends. As mentioned, at least two interpretations are possible. The poem could be viewed as an invitation to enjoy life to the fullest: "Eat, drink, and make merry, for tomorrow you may die." Or alternatively, it could represent a diatribe aimed at people who do nothing but eat, drink, and sleep. Considered in this light, the poem could conceivably represent a wake-up call rather than a general denunciation.

Unlike the previous composition, which appeals primarily to the ear, the next work appeals primarily to the eye. Although one could theoretically read it aloud, it is designed to be seen rather than heard. Indeed, if it were deprived of its visual dimension, it would be virtually impossible to decipher. Proceeding phoneme by phoneme and morpheme by morpheme, the listener would become hopelessly disoriented. By contrast, the viewer is able to grasp the poem's structure at a single glance.

a a a   a
a a   a
a   a a
a a a a

pa a ra po   a
sí a a le ra
tra   la a
ma a vras

pala raspo ma
sí aba le ras
tras   abas
ema ala as

palavraspoema
sílabasletras
letrassílabas
poemapalavras

[stanza 4: syllablesletters / letterssyllables / poemwords]

This ingenious little poem celebrates the birth of language, both spoken and written, which it reenacts symbolically. The first stanza represents the earliest phase, when our ancestors' vocabulary consisted of a few repetitive sounds. At this stage, language resembled stuttering more than speech. Thus the stanza is composed of a single vowel repeated over and over in an apparently random fashion. While primitive man is technically still inarticulate, these sounds represent an embryonic language. The vowel in question "a" will eventually assume multiple functions in Portuguese, serving as an article, a preposition, and a pronoun. During the second phase, illustrated by the next stanza, it is joined by two more vowels and seven consonants. The creation of monosyllables at this stage represents a major step in the evolution of language. If we add or subtract accents (a later development), a few simple words begin to emerge. These include the terms for "shovel" ("pá"), "frog" ("rã"), "dust" ("pó"), and "self" ("si"). The third phase, during which more letters are added, witnesses the creation of polysyllables. At this point, the conglomeration begins to look more like an actual text. Although the poem has not yet assumed its final shape, most of the syllables have been transformed into words. "Pala" means "eyeshade" (among other things); "raspo" is the first person singular of "raspar," and so forth. At this stage, the stanza reads: "eyeshade / i scrape / to me / self / skirt / he reads / ras / behind / skirts / rhea / row / ace." While the words are not arranged in any meaningful fashion, they represent an important step in the drive toward intelligibility. The ultimate breakthrough occurs in the fourth stanza, which marks the completion of this drive and the emergence of the finished poem. The final text groups words together in ways that, despite the absence of verbs, seem to make sense. In addition to language, it celebrates the phonemes, syllables, and words of which it is composed.

7
Digital Poetry

SINCE THE DEVELOPMENTS OF THE 1950S AND 1960S RECOUNTED IN the previous chapter, visual poetry has experienced a profound transformation. Like the typewriter, which helped to shape Concrete poetry, the personal computer has had a tremendous impact on contemporary visual poetry. Although some poets continue to write in the Concrete mode, many others have ventured into the virtual realm associated with recent technology. The implications of this brave new world, where visual poetry can be manipulated in a million ways, extend far beyond the domain of aesthetics. As Johanna Drucker notes, "Recent work poses profound questions about the identity of art and poetry as cultural practices and raises new questions about the processes of signification."[1] The availability of many kinds of electronic media has encouraged poets to redefine art and poetry in ways that no one could have anticipated. The numerous genres loosely classified as "media poetry" include hypertexts, kinetic poetry, video poetry, interactive poetry, animated poetry, quantum poetry, nomadic poetry, holopoetry, biopoetry, and—the subject of the present chapter—digital poetry.

Contemporary visual poems are noteworthy therefore not only for their radical vision but also for their aesthetic and intellectual sophistication. Interestingly, most are firmly grounded in critical theory. Contemporary visual poets share a fascination with electronic devices, no matter how insignificant they appear to be, and dream of creating a translinguistic language. Three of Giselle Beiguelman's nomadic poems, for example, exploit cell phones, the Internet, and Personal Digital Assistants (PDAs) respectively. "These projects," she explains, "investigate the possible realm of a post-phonetic, hybrid culture, crossed by printed and digital layers, where the informational and aesthetic codes are entangled through programming and produce a new semantics involving a rearrangement of signs and signification processes."[2] In point of fact, this description applies to a great many other visual poets as well. Most of her colleagues, including the Brazilian American poet examined below, possess similar goals and are embarked on similar programs.

EDUARDO KAC

Blessed with a fertile imagination, an impressive technical expertise, and a profound interest in the possibilities of language, Eduardo Kac has created a body of digital poetry that deserves serious attention. Since 1980 he has experimented with different media in an attempt to discover a new poetics. What made this quest so difficult, he confides, was his desire "to move beyond the limitations of the print medium and to try to think my way outside this form."[3] He not only rejected traditional poetry, in other words, but also the technology that provided it with its traditional support. Since they were the product of another age, another ethos, and another worldview, Kac felt they were hopelessly obsolete. The information age demanded a poetry that could be created and distributed over global digital networks—"an immaterial poetry" that existed only in cyberspace. Designed to be viewed either as video installations or on computers, digital poems possess a unique ontological status.[4] Like holograms, with which Kac also experimented, they can be seen but not grasped. While the eyes record what appears to be a concrete artifact, the other four senses are unable to verify its existence. A virtual construct in a world of its own making, digital poetry is situated on the divide between reality and illusion. Indeed, this paradoxical allegiance to competing perceptual systems is what gives the genre much of its appeal.

Kac's first experiment with digital poetry was entitled "Não" ("No"). Created as an ASCII composition in 1982, it was transformed into an electric signboard (LED display) two years later at the Centro Cultural Cândido Mendes in Rio de Janeiro. Passing across the screen from left to right, five blocks of letters spell out a message one by one. Consigned to a video loop, the message appears and disappears without stopping. Since by definition a loop has no end, the process could easily continue forever. Like the composition itself, the message it contains seems to be eternal. Although we normally read vertically as well as horizontally, from top to bottom and from left to right, the text is restricted to a narrow horizontal band. Three planes are superimposed on each other—or at least the illusion of three planes. Against a black background, the bright red textual blocks traverse a band of bright red dots like automobiles moving along a highway. In contrast to the message, the band itself is stationary. Composed entirely of capital letters, the five blocks are all the same length. Each possesses exactly nine letters and thus fits comfortably on the screen when it is completely assembled. Each is separated from its neighbors by two seconds as it crosses the horizontal band and occupies the screen for ten seconds from beginning to end. Among other things, the conscious symmetry and mechanical precision stress the seriousness of the poetic enterprise. This theme can be found in most, if not all, of Kac's digital poetry. In "Não" it contrasts with the precariousness of the verbal message, which is suspended in virtual space.

Deciphering the actual message proves to be surprisingly difficult. A careful reading produces the following sentence, which must be read from right to left: CORODOSIM RACONTRAO REVAIDECA ECARASEMP OPOETAESS. That the blocks of text appear in the correct order is helpful, but each one still needs to be read backwards. Not only is violating the normal reading order uncomfortable, but we have only a moment to reverse the letters in our mind before they begin to disappear. A similar difficulty exists at the level of the sentence, which, like the textual blocks, must be reversed before it can be laboriously reconstructed. Each backward block threatens to slip away before it can be deciphered and linked syntactically to the other blocks. After considerable effort, one manages to recreate the original message: OPOETAESS ECARASEMP REVAIDECA RACONTRAO CORODOSIM. As this interpretive operation suggests, Kac wants the reader/viewer to earn the poem. Instead of presenting the composition on a silver platter, he expects us to become actively involved with it. In essence, the reader/viewer is forced to recreate the work.

In order to complete this operation, however, two more obstacles remain to be overcome. To begin with, the five blocks of text are not immediately intelligible. They contain thirteen different words, parts of which combine with other words to form run-on constructions. And even if we speak Portuguese, we may not be familiar with all of the vocabulary. The problem, Kac explains, is that the poem employs slang and a funky rhythm. "Its colloquial nature was meant as a counterpoint to its digital presentation," he adds, "which, in 1982–84, felt *extremely* future-oriented, a building block in the creation of a digital culture."[5] The following translation, by the poet himself, gives a good idea of the effect he was trying to achieve: "THEPOETTH ISGUYALWA YSGOESAGA INSTTHECO YYESCHOIR." In other words, however we choose to conceive the poet, he is first and foremost a rebel—someone who refuses to be bound either by tradition or by convention. Since he insists on going his own way, the poet is essentially a loner. His favorite reply when "the yes choir" asks him to join them is an emphatic "Não!"

"Reabracadabra" is a videotext animated poem that was shown in 1985 in the group exhibition "Arte On-Line" in São Paulo. In contrast to the previous composition, which was concerned with words, it is obsessed with letters. Superimposed on a black background, a small, green equilateral triangle gradually takes shape, descending from top to bottom. This figure is gradually enclosed by a larger green triangle that descends the page in the same manner; following a green rectangle then appears toward the bottom of the large triangle. Next, a yellow wave of color washes over the entire structure. As the green lines are replaced by yellow lines, descending from top to bottom, the structure suddenly becomes three-dimensional and is transformed into a large capital A. Thereafter a number of white dots surround the monumental letter and slowly become tiny letters. The sequence ERCDDBY is repeated twice before the letters disappear, one by one, leaving the dots shimmering against the black background. As they begin to vanish, a black curtain descends and covers everything.

The question that naturally arises at this point is how to interpret this intriguing composition. Like "Não," "Reabracadabra" is concerned with the way things suddenly appear and disappear. Also like "Não," it proceeds with mechanical precision from start to finish but does not continue. The final curtain is precisely that—final. The progression from green to yellow to red, the reverse of their order in the spectrum, appears to be significant. Like a traffic light, it reflects the three stages of the present journey: its beginning, middle, and end. However, what are we to make of all the letters in the poem? And what role does the large A play? Kac's explanation is succinct and to the point: "An incantatory word of Kabalistic resonance is rendered as a cosmic monolith following the atomic model (the vowel as nucleus and the consonants as orbiting particles)" (EKAC). In the beginning, it seems, was the vowel, which occupies the center of the alphabetic universe, according to the poet. The large A is so powerful that it functions as an "incantatory word"—like the biblical word made flesh. By comparison, the consonants are merely attendants, assigned to care for this central figure.

The word "abracadabra," one should add, is a magical incantation dating from the second century AD. "It was usually inscribed inside an inverted triangle," one authority explains, "or was set out so that it formed [an inverted triangle]."[6] In "Reabracadabra," of course, it assumes the form of an upright triangle. Added to the original incantation, the prefix "re-" suggests that the poem contains a double transformation. The title may allude to the triangle's magical appearance and disappearance. Or, more likely, to the triangle's appearance and subsequent transformation into a capital A. Some specialists maintain that "abracadabra" originally meant "I will create, as I say," others that it signifies "What was said has been done." In either case, the expression retains its original sense today. To a prestidigitator it means the same thing as "presto change-o." Interestingly, an implicit parallel exists between the magician and Kac himself in this poem. Both individuals are concerned with the world of illusion; both seem able to perform miracles.

The next work to emerge from the poet's fertile brain was entitled "OCO" ("HOLLOW"). Conceived as an interactive holopoem in 1985, it was recreated five years later as an interactive digital poem. Although the latter utilizes capital letters like the two previous works, it bears no resemblance to them. A wholly original creation, it marks a brand new departure. The letters in question, which fill most of the screen, are large, gray, and three-dimensional. Spelling out the title, O, C, and O are arranged to form an imaginary tube, imaginary because they are separated from each other by the same distance as their width. Despite their tubular construction, they could never hold gas or water. As the imaginary creation whirls this way and that, the letter I appears from time to time and enters the tube. Once again, the poet's commentary proves to be invaluable. "'OCO' explores the three-dimensional architecture of these letters," Kac confides, "and the multiple meanings that emerge when the letter I appears and disappears rhythmically in virtual space" (MP, 54). "OCIO," he goes on to explain, means "leisure" but also "immobility" and "laziness." O basically serves as an article. "CIO" means something like "rut" or "arousal." And besides "hollow," "OCO" can signify "futile," "vain," or "insignificant." Slowly a picture begins to emerge that is supported by the crude sexual symbolism depicted visually. The composition evokes an indolent, vain, and superficial couple engaged in sexual intercourse. The rhythm of the gyrating letters matches the rhythm of their lovemaking, pausing once or twice and then accelerating toward the end.

Another animated videotext, "Tesão," was shown in 1986 at the group exhibition Brazil High-Tech in São Paulo. Compared to the previous works, which are relatively sedate, "Tesão" seems positively flashy. Not only does the composition make use of six different colors, but the colors are constantly changing. A red line is followed by a green line that is followed by a yellow line, and so forth. By far the most colorful of Kac's digital experiments, it is divided into three distinct movements. While each of these possesses its own unique characteristics, each advances at the same deliberate pace and lasts the same amount of time (approximately sixty-five seconds). The first movement incorporates three up-and-down motions: from the top of the screen to the bottom, from the bottom back to the top, and from the top back to the bottom. A red inverted V descends the screen, acquiring a yellow crossbar in the process. A vertical green line sprouts from each of its two extremities and rises straight up. A V descends from each of the green extremities and acquires a pink crossbar. Following the appearance of a large yellow square, which is superimposed on the previous figures, a black curtain descends and covers everything. While this is both entertaining and technically accomplished, one wonders what it all signifies. Fortunately, Kac provides the missing key. "Words emerge and disappear through layers of lines and color masses," he declares, "forming an ephemeral digital graffiti" (EKAC). And sure enough, upon (re) examination, the movement turns out to contain three letters: A, M, and O.

Now that we know what to look for, we are prepared to investigate the second movement, which resembles the first in several respects. It begins with a large red V, for example, which gradually descends to the bottom of the screen. Next, a green square is superimposed on the capital V, which, as we have seen, represents the letter O. Finally, a blue curved line inscribes itself within the square, followed by a large orange E that is positioned in the center. According to all indications, the second movement contains four letters: V, O, C, and Ê. The final section is characterized by a veritable explosion of color. Whereas the first two movements are linear constructions, these are replaced by the subtle play of volumes. Somewhat unexpectedly, Kac abandons drawing in favor of painting. Because he proceeds by superimposing blocks of color, this makes the letters more difficult to detect. Each of the blocks fills most of the (black) screen and descends from top to bottom until it is complete. Since each is a little smaller than its predecessor, the latter is never completely effaced. Beginning with a large orange block, the poet superimposes blue, yellow, pink, and green blocks, in that order. Since the process is cumulative, traces of each step are still visible at the end.

Not until we have finished viewing the third movement, perhaps, do we notice that each of the blocks forms a highly stylized letter. The visual clues tend to be fairly subtle. In retrospect, however, the section contains the following five letters: T, E, S, Ã, and O. At last we are in a position to reconstruct the fragmentary sentence that lies just beneath the composition's surface: "AMO VOCÊ TESÃO." As Kac pointed out in a conversation with the author, this expression can be translated in two different ways. First of all, it can be understood as an expression of affection: "I LOVE YOU" followed by what the speaker feels, which he chooses to translate as "HORNINESS" ("tesão" is the common Brazilian word for "erection"). Secondly, the term can represent a passionate compliment blurted out during lovemaking. In either case, the woman to whom the message was addressed clearly aroused strong feelings in the poet. The decision to incorporate this sentence into the composition was risky, to say the least. In transgressing the boundary between private and public, Kac exposed himself to possible public ridicule and worse. "Anybody could see it," he recalls, "as these online terminals were available in shopping malls, libraries, schools, etc., and the exhibition was highly publicized." But of course it would be a mistake to focus exclusively on the verbal message. After all, this is primarily a visual composition. Much of what the poem communicates stems from its rhythm, its animation, its visual transitions, and the contrast between line and volume.

Like the previous poem, "Recaos" ("Re-chaos") was shown at the Brazil High-Tech exhibition in 1986. Another videotext animation, it presents an apocalyptic vision of the end of the world. More precisely, it evokes a return to chaos, to the primordial soup from which the universe was formed. Materializing in the lower right-hand corner, the letter C generates an A and then a string of O's that are projected diagonally, one after the other, toward the top left-hand corner. Striking the upper edge of the screen, they ricochet downward and encounter the left edge, where they rebound once again. Transformed into a string of S's, they rocket across the screen horizontally, traverse the initial stream of letters, and halt at the right edge. Up to this point all of the letters have been red. As soon as the S's reach the right margin, however, three letters turn blue where the two strings intersect and spell out "SOS." Unfortunately, it is far too late for anyone to come to our rescue; the universe is already disintegrating. Like the letters forming the word "caos," which are trapped in a cosmic pinball game, we are no longer masters of our destiny. As the composition evolves, Kac points out, it leaves "a mnemonic trace of other words such as 'so' ('alone') and 'ossos' ('bones')" (*MP,* 52). While the first word describes our deplorable situation, the second evokes our ultimate fate. In addition, the composition concludes with two poignant icons. Kac identifies the final visual configuration as both a bottomless hour-glass and the symbol of infinity. The first image stresses the fact that time is running out; the second that we will return to the vacant and infinite space that preceded the birth of the universe.

Like the previous two works, "Deus" ("God") was exhibited at the Brazil High-Tech show in 1986. And like them, it is a videotext animation. To be sure, a great many poems exist that celebrate the glory of God. There are even visual poems, such as George Herbert's "Easter Wings," that fit this description. Although the title "Deus" leads one to expect something similar, the composition is far from a religious experience. Initially, a large white rectangle descends from top to bottom, covering much of the black screen. Next, seventeen vertical bars of varying thicknesses descend from the top of the horizontal rectangle to the bottom. Thereafter, apparently random letters and numbers appear in the narrow space beneath the bars. They do not all appear at the same time, however, but in four stages. First "19" appears on the left and "86" on the right. Then a 6 is added to the first group: "19 6" and a 4 to the second group: "4 86." Next, each of the vacant spaces receives a letter: "19D6" and "4S86." And finally an additional letter appears: "19D6E" and "U4S86." Disguised as a bar code, the composition looks perfectly convincing. Upon closer inspection, however, one discovers that it contains two "mistakes." Real bar codes do not have letters at the bottom, only numbers. And some of the letters in Kac's version spell recognizable words. In its final form, the alphanumeric sequence contains a proper noun and a pronoun: "DEUS" and "EU" ("I"). Because of his ability to create an (aesthetic) object ex nihilo, the poet seems to be saying, he resembles God. Within the confines of a specific work of art, his power is absolute. Interestingly, the numbers at the bottom of the "bar code" are not random, either. The first numbers to appear—"19 86"—indicate the date that the work was produced. Like a true artist, Kac has dated and signed his composition.

One of the poet's most beguiling compositions is entitled "IO." A three-dimensional navigational poem created in 1990, it was translated into VRML (Virtual Reality Mark-Up Language) five years later. On the one hand, as Kac states, the work is devoted to the "exploration of the virtual architecture of the letter." On the other hand, since "IO" means "I" in Italian, it is also concerned with the exploration of the self. These twin goals are not irreconcilable, the poet adds, because "the self is presented as an inexhaustible navigational field." Although one of Jupiter's moons is also named Io, neither it nor the mythological character whose name it bears appear to figure in the poem. Instead, Kac explains that the

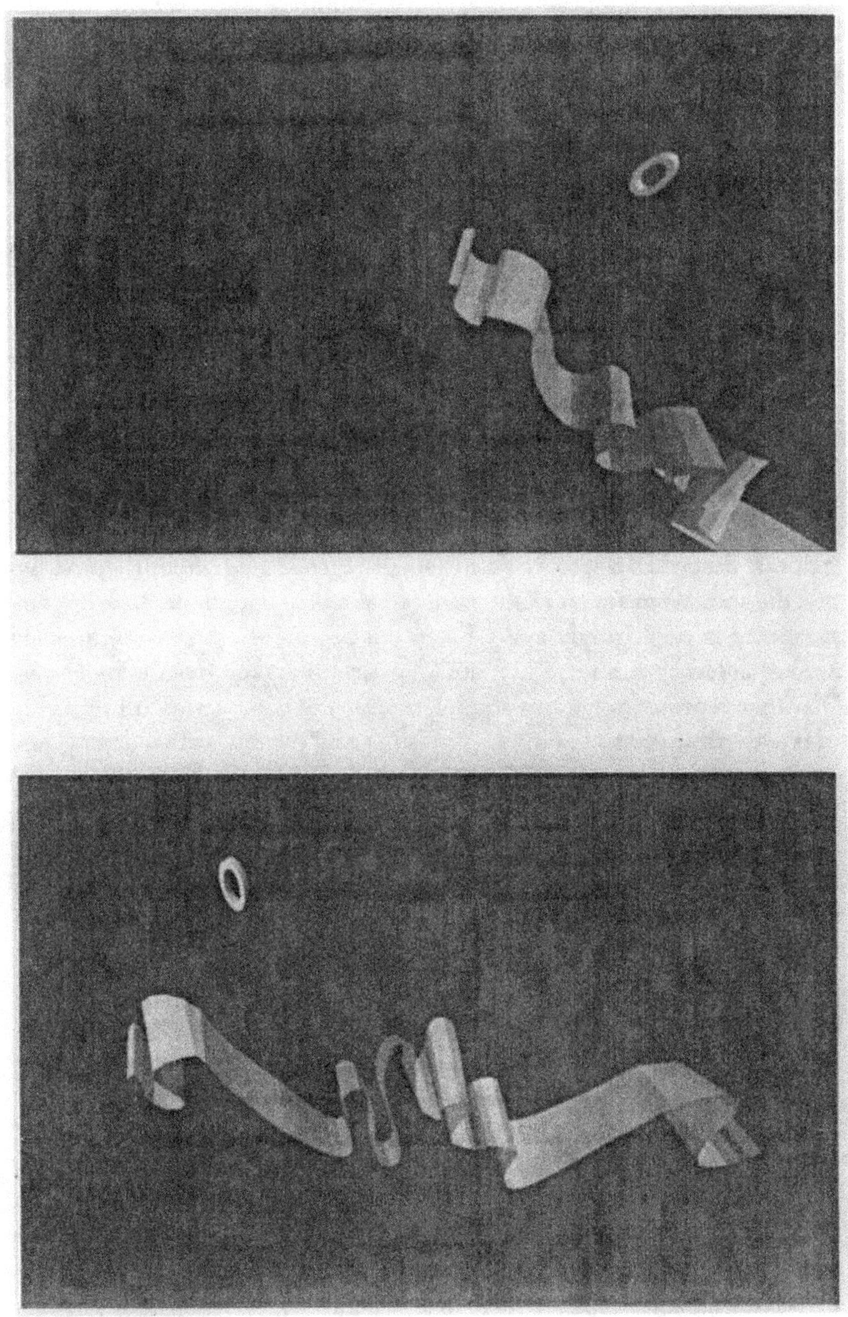

18. Eduardo Kac, "IO"

letters I and O, which also represent the numbers one and zero, function as elements of an imaginary landscape. In addition, they stand for "reconciled differences" between such conceptual antagonists as one and zero, line and circle, and so forth. Like the Surrealists before him, Kac invokes the ancient alchemical principle of *coincidencia oppositorum,* that is to say, the union of opposites. Readers are invited, he concludes, "to explore the space (up/down, left/right, forward/backward) created by the stylized letters and experience it both as an abstract environment and as a visual text" (MP, 55).

In contrast to their normal existence on the printed page, the letters/numbers in the composition are solidly three-dimensional. One is reminded of the advent of 3-D movies in the 1950s. Like the filmmakers of that period, Kac goes to considerable lengths to show what his marvelous new medium can do. Projected against the utter blackness of outer space, the I becomes a long pink ribbon which, in contrast to the letter (or number) itself, is amazingly supple. Rippling and curling as it moves through space, it describes a series of arabesques. Pirouetting about the first figure, the somewhat smaller O is rendered as a blue doughnut. Like its companion, it is surprisingly agile. From the beginning, the two figures are accompanied by a tiny yellow dot—apparently taken from a lower case "i"—that represents the sun shining millions of miles away. All three figures are extraordinarily mobile—twisting and turning as the virtual camera zooms in on, or pulls back from, a particular shape. Halfway through the performance, for example, it zooms in on the sun so close that the picture is too large for the screen. Elegantly choreographed from beginning to end, the performance concludes with the principal dancers positioned side by side and the sun once again reduced to the size of a dot.

Created in 1994, "Accident" is the first of the digital poems to be endowed with a sound track. "An investigation of the infinite loop as a poetic rhythm," Kac explains, "this poem is about accidents of language, possible misunderstandings, and the lack of need of language when two lovers meet in their embrace" (MP, 57). As such, it repeats a single, haunting phrase over and over: "The words won't come out right." The composition not only describes the problem in question, therefore, but performs it before our very eyes. In theory, the repetition is supposed to take place at both the sonic and the iconic levels, both of which are subject to violent distortions. However, the sound track consists entirely of mysterious gurgles and rasping noises, none of which resemble human speech. Thus it falls to the visual message, printed in white against a black background, to carry the semantic load. The latter consists of three attempts to reproduce the phrase, only two of which are successful. As the distortion increases, the words on the screen are buffeted about as if by gusts of wind. The first attempt to communicate the message encounters no resistance. Warped by mysterious forces, the second is barely successful. The third attempt only manages to reproduce a few letters and syllables before dissolving into a fine mist. Although this scenario can be repeated again and again, the words will never come out right. By contrast, Kac declares, people in love do not need words to express themselves. "A lover's discourse," he observes, "is made of physical contact, gazes and gestures" (MP, 57). For that matter, he adds, the visual image might even depict two people vigorously making love. "Accident" does not proclaim the failure of language, in any case, but rather its inadequacy to express certain things. As such, it dramatizes the limitations of speech.

"UPC" was created the same year as the preceding poem. At first, it seems to have been a video installation in which seven-foot letters were projected against the wall. At some point, however, Kac decided to combine video projection with an electronic signboard. As orange lights flash a continuous message, a band of letters emerges from the right rear, crosses the black screen diagonally, and disappears at the front left. Although the band is two-dimensional, like that in "Não," it seems to pass through three-dimensional space. Taller than the spectators, the letters traverse the screen at a brisk pace and are gone almost before we can make out the words: "NOTHING ABOVE TO LEFT OR RIGHT NOTHING BELOW."

This message is repeated three times, with a brief black space between the repetitions. As the third repetition ends, the message reappears in a subdued black-and-white video and crosses the screen at a different angle. Although it is displayed on the same electronic sign, the lights have become blurry pastels. The virtual camera zooms in so far that everything is out of focus. Following a brief blackout, the camera zooms back out, reversing the sequence we have just witnessed. The original orange message reappears, followed by the subdued black-and-white video again, which is followed by the orange message once more. All of a sudden, the scene changes, and a smaller black-and-white video projects the familiar message onto a movie screen in a room somewhere. A man and a woman are watching it with their backs turned toward us. For a moment, an excerpt from the subdued black-and-white version is superimposed on their backs. As the movie screen message is about to conclude, the original black-and-white video returns, the virtual camera zooms in again, and the composition ends in a flurry of hazy pastels.

Since "UPC" is also equipped with a sound track, it operates on two levels simultaneously. While our eyes are following the complex visual scenario, our ears are attuned to its sonic dimension. In contrast to the former, which is highly structured, the sound track consists of random sounds presumably recorded at the original exhibition. Numerous spectators can be heard making all the little sounds normally associated with a crowd, including talking, walking, and occasional coughing. The constant background echo suggests that the installation is in a cavernous hall. A few voices are loud, but all of them are muffled. Although we are aware of the visitors, we cannot see them or understand them. Like us, who are spectators too, they participate in the composition but remain invisible throughout. Since the poem seems to be about space, or rather about the illusion of space, this makes a certain amount of sense.

To be sure, the mysterious message is hopelessly ambiguous. It could be a judgment, a preference, or an evaluation. It could refer to the marketplace, to politics, or to aesthetics. Or it could simply describe the message's spatial orientation. Suspended in space, the words are completely isolated. There is nothing above, below, or on either side of it except darkness. The message bears an eerie resemblance to the earth itself which is surrounded by the vast inky blackness of space. And that brings us to a related theme: the difficulty of situating oneself without reference to external coordinates. Like Russian dolls that fit one inside the other, the composition employs a nesting structure. The two people watching the video on the movie screen are in a video themselves, and we are watching it. In this role, they mirror our own position as spectators, and vice versa. Perhaps we are the subjects of a video as well—there is no way of knowing.

Composed in 1995, "Insect. Desperto" ("Insect. Awake") is a run-time animation, like several of the previous poems. As the title implies, it is a bilingual composition, combining an English text with a Portuguese sound track. While the visual and sonic elements complement each other, each track is essentially independent. The text consists of twenty-three words repeated over and over according to several patterns. Printed in large, white letters on a black background, they appear at different places on the screen and last for only a fraction of a second. The first word appears in the upper left-hand corner, for example, the second at the lower left, the third at the upper right, and the fourth at the lower right. "The elusive movements of the words on the screen," Kac declares, "can be seen as unresolved hesitations concerning the construction of syntagms. They can also be seen as reflecting the fleeting behavior of flying insects. In either case, both are meant to evoke inconsistencies and undecided aspects of life" (MP, 57–58). In either case, the frenetic visual rhythm contrasts with the calm, soothing rhythm of the spoken words, which sound as if they were recorded in an echo chamber. Some visual sequences progress in a clockwise direction, some move counterclockwise, and some choose different paths altogether. As soon as a recognizable pattern is established, it immediately changes. Each of the eight sequences begins with the same word, which appears in the upper left-hand corner: "close up." The first three sequences are identical:

> close up unclear nonsense awake in the dark
> helpless insects I hold I uncover far far away
> clear skies clear like targets open opaque abysm

The fourth series, twice as long, follows the same progression, and then reverses it when it reaches the end. The next three sequences adopt the backward version, regressing from "abysm" to "unclear." As Kac points out, these reversals open new possibilities of signification (MP, 57), but the final series returns to the initial model. The text concludes with the word "abysm" centered in the middle of the screen, which then fades away. Whereas many of the other compositions begin all over again, "Insect. Desperto" simply ends. "This is meant to stress the linearity of the experience," Kac explains, "and at the same time to undermine it" (MP, 57). The text itself is extremely fragmented. Words follow words with no punctuation and no appreciable syntax to tie them together. And yet, they seem to follow a certain nightmarish logic—at least in the initial sequence. Indeed, with a little effort one can reconstruct a plausible scenario. The narrator is suddenly awakened in the middle of the night by some horrible insects. Perhaps hungry mosquitoes have invaded the room, or perhaps cockroaches are crawling on the bed. For reasons that are unclear (but no less terrifying), it is not possible to get rid of them. The narrator is completely helpless. At this point, the initial sense of desperation is replaced by another, calmer mood. Hoping to be saved, in the double sense of the word, the narrator turns his eyes toward heaven. Since everyone wants to go there when they die, he compares heaven to a celestial target. Entering paradise, he adds, is like entering a divine abyss, which opens to admit the chosen few but whose depths are shrouded in mist.

These concerns are reflected in the spoken narrative that accompanies the visual text:

de perto nada é tão certo
dentro tudo é escuro
desperto mas insensato
indefeso feito inseto indefeso
resguardo o que é tão caro
descobro aquilo que espero
ao longe onde o céu é tão claro
claro
como se o nada
fosse o alvo
o alvo abismo aberto

[nearby nothing is so certain / within everything is dark / awake but unclear / helpless done insect helpless / protection that which is so dear / I discover that which I hope for / far away where the sky is so clear / clear / as if nothingness / were the target / the target open abysm]

The composition "addresses the differences between spoken and written languages," Kac explains, "exploring distinct possibilities unique to these semiotic systems" (MP, 57). The Portuguese version not only benefits from the language's sonorous qualities but also from several internal rhymes. Although there are obvious differences between the spoken and the written texts, the similarities are rather striking. The sound track possesses the same structure and the same themes as the visual track. Some of the words are even identical, including the Portuguese terms for "awake," "unclear," "dark," "helpless," "insect," "sky," "far away," "clear," "targets," "open," and "abysm." While we don't know which served as the original model, the two versions are clearly closely related. Although the spoken and the written texts develop in quite different ways, they coincide briefly toward the end of the poem. As the word "abysm" flashes on the screen, we hear the Brazilian speaker say "abismo." As the English term fades away, he adds one more word: "aberto."

As Kac declares, "Wine" (1996) is a delicate and silent animation poem. "It suggests an inebriate mental state," he adds, "in which foreground and background blend in almost undifferentiated fashion" (MP, 62). In keeping with his oenological agenda, the poet chose an appropriate color scheme. Superimposed on a bright red background, the (handwritten) words are the color of burgundy. As in the previous poem, they appear in unexpected places, linger briefly, then vanish. Words even give birth to other words, which emerge full-blown from their verbal chrysalis. In general, they conform to the following scenario: entering from the right, the expression "at times" appears in the lower right-hand corner, followed by "the wind" at the upper left, which suddenly materializes. Then "at times" disappears, and "the wind" replicates itself below. Moving toward the right, each of the twin expressions expands to read "through the wind," with the upper words superimposed on the lower ones. Changing places with each other, each of the two expressions is transformed into "the window." Next, the word "blows" enters from the lower left, generates "i look," and disappears. Superimposed on "i look," "i go" moves toward the right and vanishes. Gradually materializing in the center of the screen, four identical instances of "at times" overlap and then disappear. Entering from the lower right, the words "but ages ago" appear and then fade away. Thus the basic text appears to read:

> at times the wind through the wind the window
> blows i look i go at times but ages ago

"The word 'window' acts as a central metaphor," Kac explains, "as it suggests the separation between internal and external spaces (both on mental and physical levels). It alludes both to the physical and the computer window. The 'verbal wind' penetrates both spaces and flows in both directions. The poem communicates as much through the verbal apparitions as it does through their carefully orchestrated evanescence" (MP, 62).

Two remaining digital compositions are not only ingenious but surprisingly sophisticated. Created in 1996, "Letter" is a 3-D interactive poem that resembles a tapered beer glass. Like a twelve-ounce pilsner glass, it consists of a flat, round base (a two-dimensional spiral) attached to a cone (a three-dimensional spiral). Both portions are composed of strings of words. Since the reader/viewer can manipulate the poem at will, he or she can view it from every conceivable angle. One can even fly through the composition, if one wishes, or circle it like a bird. Although the cone may seem alternatively to converge on and to emerge from the flat disc, the words tell a different story. The stream of sentences begins at the bottom of the cone and spirals up to the top. Seen upside down and backwards, the sentences are admittedly difficult to reconstruct. With a little effort, however, one can make out the last two sentences: "Last year when she visited I asked her to bring an old album of photographs. I could remember stories of joy, of pain, of aging, of survival." Similarly, the flat spiral forming the base reads: "When she came out it was the most incredible moment. I ran to make sure she was OK

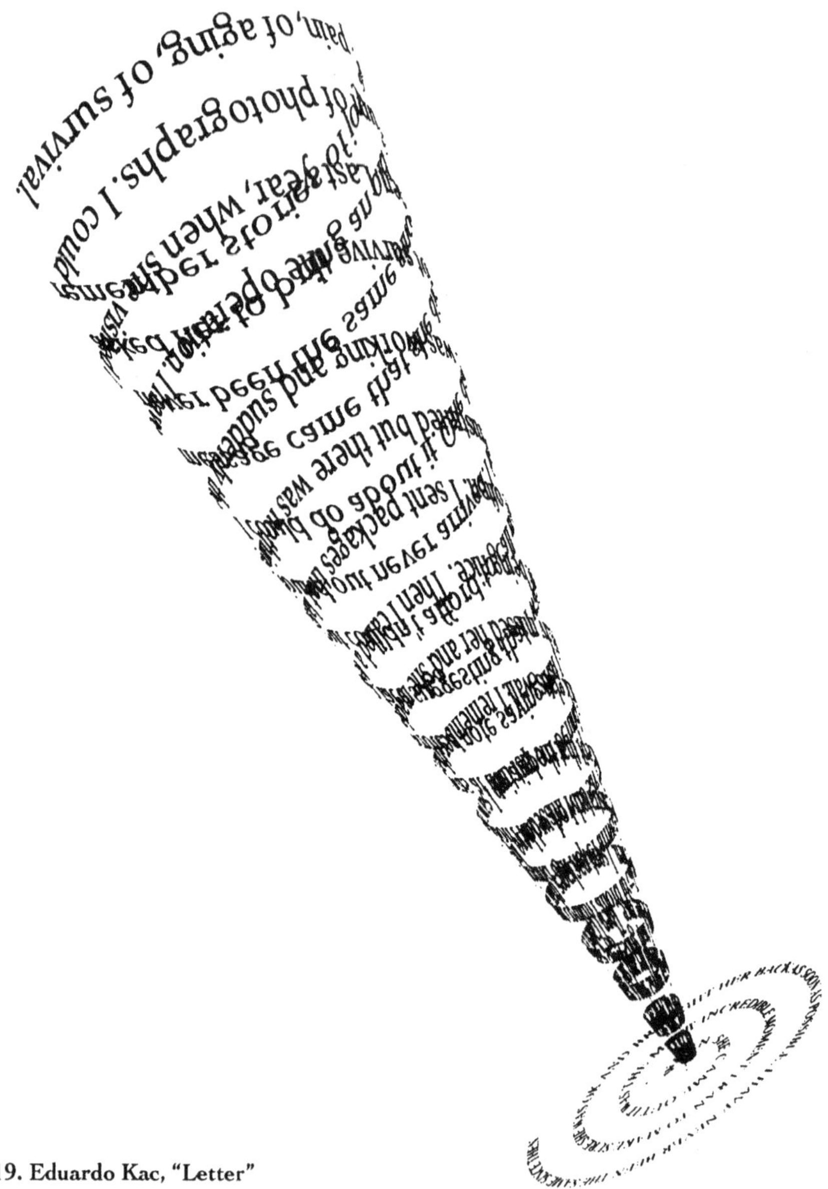

19. Eduardo Kac, "Letter"

and brought her back as soon as possible. I have never been the same since then." Like these examples, Kac confides, the other sentences are supposedly fragments of letters written to the same person. In addition, the different subjects are conflated into a single addressee (MP, 62). If one devoted enough time and energy to the project, one could presumably decipher the entire composition. However, there really is little point in recording every single sentence. What matters is not the details but rather Kac's broader mission. Containing poignant memories of his grandmother, his mother, and his daughter, "Letter" celebrates their existence, past and present.

With "Reversed Mirror" (1997), Kac entered a very different domain, one that presented brand-new challenges to his digital imagination. This was the domain of trance poetry. Conceived as a digital videopoem, the composition records "the subtle dissolution and reconfiguration of verbal particles, [and] is charged with a feeling that is at once calm and vibrant" (MP, 62). The source of this contradictory feeling is not hard to locate. The musical sound track that accompanies the poem is slow and fast at the same time. Played on an electric piano, or perhaps a harmonium, eight notes are calmly repeated over and over. Each repetition consists of five notes followed by a pause and then by three more notes. The effect is extremely hypnotic. At the same time, a percussion instrument maintains a rapid beat that both complements and conflicts with this hypnotic style. During the first half, this role is played by a drum that sounds something like a tabla. During the remainder of the composition, the first instrument is replaced by vague accordionlike sounds and the second by another drum and rapid brushwork. As before, the music is highly repetitive, and the tension continues to exist between the two tempos.

At first, the visual images are hopelessly indistinct. Gray shadows against a white background vibrate up and down in time to the rapid beat. Gradually growing larger and larger, they eventually metamorphose into individual letters, which are superimposed on abstract shapes. Since the letters only approximate their true forms, and since they continue to vibrate up and down, they are difficult to identify. The same is true of the words they spell out. As soon as each word reaches its full size, the process is reversed, and it begins to grow smaller and smaller. All that remains after it has disappeared is a series of abstract shapes vibrating in time with the music. This process continues until all the words have materialized, have been recorded, and have vanished. "Through its peculiar rhythm," Kac declares, the work "articulates the notion that language (particularly written language) is in fact nothing but a transitional moment in a much more complex semiological continuum" (MP, 62). Language comprises not just marks on the page, or sounds in the mouth, but the process of signification itself. Words inhabit a whole spectrum of possibilities from the moment they are conceived to the moment they are formed and the moment they cease to exist. Even then, they are preserved as virtual constructs in our memory. Thus language resembles a living organism whose traces remain with us indefinitely.

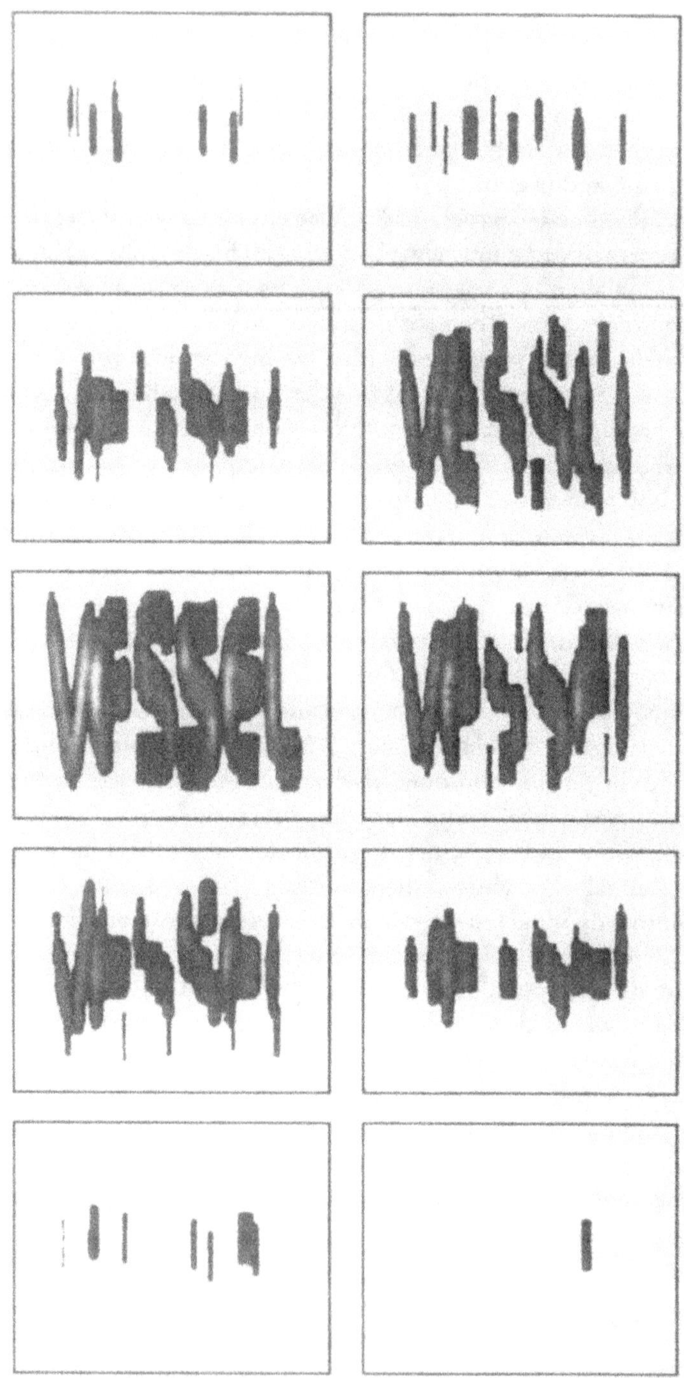

20. Eduardo Kac, "Reversed Mirror"

"Reversed Mirror" is not just concerned with how words behave, however, but also with what they say. While the poem demonstrates language in action, it also comments on the world around us. Or rather, it comments on our perception of the world around us. Once again, as the title reveals, reality is contrasted with illusion, and vice versa. Turning our attention to the words that have gradually emerged in the course of the poem, we encounter the message:

REVERSED VESSEL IN A TRANSVERSE
UNIVERSE MIRROR IN A MIRROR
WATCHES A MIRROR IN A MIRROR

The first two words appear initially to describe a glass or a bowl that has been turned upside down. After a certain amount of delay, however, one realizes they refer to something entirely different. Comparing the two words to the poem's title, one suddenly realizes the vessel is a metaphor for the mirror. Since the latter can be said to contain an image, it is portrayed here as a container. The reversed vessel is a reversed mirror, and vice versa. But what exactly is a reversed mirror? How are we to understand this curious reference? Since a mirror normally presents a reversed image, a reversed mirror would seem to be one in which the image is *not* reversed. But how does one reverse an image in a mirror? Is such a thing even possible? And what is a transverse universe? Since the universe radiates out in every direction simultaneously, it is difficult to see how it could extend crosswise. Be that as it may, the remainder of the message contains the answer to the previous question. The way to reverse an image in a mirror is to incorporate a second mirror into the first. Or rather to incorporate the *image* of a second mirror into the first. The trick is to place the second mirror so that it reflects the original image back into the original mirror, where the reversed image will be reversed again and will thus appear normal. The infinite regression that Kac envisages could theoretically extend forever. Placed opposite each other, two mirrors with unreversed images would present reversed images of each other, which according to the same operation would be transformed into unreversed images, then reversed images, and so forth, ad infinitem. Like reality, it turns out, truth is hard to separate from illusion. The virtual world is a complicated place, where nothing is necessarily what it seems.

8
Eyesight and Insight

As THE PREVIOUS CHAPTERS HAVE DEMONSTRATED, VISUAL POETRY possesses an impressive range of achievements. At the verbal level, it is capable of complex formulations, striking observations, and unsuspected nuances. At the visual level, it assumes a great many guises, from minimalist exercises to rapid sketches, schematic drawings, poster poems, and full-fledged pictures. Although traditional poetry also possesses a visual dimension, we are not normally aware of it. We read through the material text to the meaning that lies beyond it. The words on the page are essentially invisible. Since their sole function is to convey meaning, they serve as signs rather than as icons. By contrast, visual poems call attention to their physical attributes. As Johanna Drucker observes, their self-conscious materiality signifies that they are associated with being rather than with representing.[1] They possess the same ontological status as objects. In contrast to traditional poetry, moreover, the visual elements participate in the construction of the total composition. As modern advertising has been quick to realize, fully integrated verbal and visual elements multiply the possibilities of meaning.

Writing in 1969, Rudolf Arnheim differentiated between two kinds of perceptual thinking in art, which he identified as intellectual and intuitive cognition, respectively.[2] Whereas intellectual perception concerns itself with verbal categories, he explained, intuitive perception focuses on visual patterns. Arnheim's perceptive insights, which drew on gestalt psychology, have since been confirmed by neuroscientists. Research conducted mainly by R. W. Sperry and his students at Cal Tech has revealed that the two halves of the brain possess different cognitive modes. "The left hemisphere is verbal and analytic," Betty Edwards reports, "while that of the right is nonverbal and global."[3] The differences between the two halves turn out to be quite striking. The left brain behaves in a rational, sequential, and objective manner, J. E. Bogen explains, while the right brain acts intuitively, simultaneously, and subjectively. In contrast to the former mode, which is linear, analytic, and abstract, the second is nonlinear, holistic, and concrete.[4] Extrapolating from this model, the distinction between intellectual and intuitive would seem to apply to literature and art, each of which demands a different cognitive approach. At the very least, it describes how visual poetry operates. That words and sentences appeal to the reader's intellect comes as no surprise. As soon as the latter perceives them, he or she translates them into a series of concepts. That paintings appeal to the viewer's intuitive nature is not surprising, either. Much of the latter's response to art assumes the form of unconscious impressions. What makes the foregoing model so important is the realization that visual stimuli are associated with cognition.

Throughout history, visual perception has been viewed essentially as a passive response. Following the invention of photography, people began to compare the eye to a camera, and vice versa. Expressions such as "the camera eye" have perpetuated this analogy ever since.[5] In reality, of course, vision is far more complicated than the comparison suggests. In addition to recording visual impulses, the eye transmits these impulses to the brain, which must immediately decide how to interpret them. Most of the time, the brain experiences little difficulty. Drawing on past experience, it translates the impulses into a mental picture. Occasionally, the brain does not recognize the original image or is unable to choose between competing interpretations. This situation arises with multistable images, such as Wittgenstein's famous duck-rabbit drawing or the vase framed by two faces cited by Edwards, both of which encourage contradictory readings.[6] Whereas the first drawing portrays two animals simultaneously, the second depicts a vase first and then two faces, as the viewer's focus shifts from figure to ground. Negative space is translated into positive space as control shifts from the left hemisphere to the right hemisphere. In both drawings, the brain repeatedly analyzes the visual impulses and tries to integrate them into a single recognizable image. What this means, Arnheim rightfully concludes, is that "visual perception is visual thinking."[7] Like its companion, the right hemisphere employs a high-level cognitive mode "which involves [unconscious] thinking, reasoning, and complex mental functioning."[8]

In addition to constructing a mental image, the brain has to ascertain what that image means. Whether these operations take place simultaneously, as seems probable, or sequentially makes little difference. At some point the brain needs to create an image, identify it, and determine its significance. Unlike the ocean or a spectacular sunset, a visual poem does not belong to the natural world. Like the text, the design is suspended in space and time between two different people. According to the well-known semiotic model, the artist codes the picture in the first place, and the viewer decodes it subsequently. The problem with this metaphor is that it reduces visual perception to a passive role instead of an active exploration. What actually happens, as we have just seen, is that the viewer mentally recreates the original picture. In a certain sense, the viewer becomes an artist himself. As Arnheim declares, "Every man's eyesight anticipates in a modest way the justly admired capacity of the artist to produce patterns that validly interpret experience by means of organized form. Eyesight is insight."[9] For critics of visual poetry, the last statement rings especially true. Like literary texts, in any case, visual creations interpret the world in which we live. Literature proceeds intellectually, and art proceeds intuitively. In addition, each has an important aesthetic function to fulfill. Visual poetry derives its distinctiveness from its simultaneous participation in both worlds. Scientists postulate that the nature of the operation to be accomplished determines which of the brain's hemispheres will take charge. Normally one hemisphere overrides the other, preventing or inhibiting it from functioning. The genius of visual poetry is that it appeals to *both* sides of the brain, integrating intellectual and intuitive experience into a complex whole. Wedded both to literature and to art, it produces insights and aesthetic experiences that few other genres can equal.

Notes

Chapter 1: Word Made Flesh

1. François Rigolot, "Le Poétique et l'analogique," *Poétique,* no. 35 (September 1978): 267–68.

2. Willard Bohn, *Modern Visual Poetry* (Newark: University of Delaware Press, 2001), 16–17.

3. The Poem Generator, www.vita.uwnet.nl/poem/poem.html.

4. The Sackner Archive of Concrete and Visual Poetry, www.rediscov.com/sackner archives/.

5. Marjorie Perloff, *Radical Artifice: Writing Poetry in the Age of Media* (Chicago: University of Chicago Press, 1991), 93.

6. Rudolf Arnheim, *Art and Visual Perception: A Psychology of the Creative Eye,* rev. ed. (Berkeley: University of California Press, 1974), 42–46.

7. W. J. T. Mitchell, *What Do Pictures Want?: The Lives and Loves of Images* (Chicago: University of Chicago Press, 2005), xvii.

8. Ibid., 188–96.

9. Rudolf Arnheim, *Visual Thinking* (Berkeley: University of California Press, 1969), 135–52.

Chapter 2: Spanish Ultraist Poetry

1. Rafael Cansinos-Asséns, *La nueva literatura* (Madrid: Paéz, 1927), 3:195.

2. Guillermo de Torre, *Guillaume Apollinaire: estudio preliminar y páginas escogidas* (Buenos Aires: Poseidon, 1946), 20.

3. René de Costa, "Trayectoria del caligrama en Huidobro," *Poesía* (Madrid), no. 3 (November-December 1978): 36.

4. See *Dada Almanach,* ed. Richard Huelsenbeck (Berlin: Reiss, 1920), 156.

5. I am indebted to Yasbel Fernández-Acuña for this insight.

6. For an analysis of Apollinaire's "Paysage," see Bohn, *Modern Visual Poetry,* 100–121.

7. For an analysis of "Signo celeste," see Willard Bohn, *The Aesthetics of Visual Poetry, 1914–1928* (Cambridge: Cambridge University Press, 1986; Chicago: University of Chicago Press, 1993), 163–67.

8. Gloria Videla, *El Ultraísmo,* 2nd ed. (Madrid: Gredos, 1971), 165.

9. See Ernst Robert Curtius, *European Literature and the Latin Middle Ages*, tr. Willard Trask (New York: Harper and Row, 1953), 120 and 185ff.

10. See Bohn, *Aesthetics of Visual Poetry*, 146–71. Although it does not seem to have attracted any imitators, a visual composition by Paul Morand appeared in *Grecia* on June 10, 1919, translated by Rafael Cansinos-Asséns. Entitled "Antología: en la Puerta del Sol," it juxtaposed numerous signs from the Spanish square to make an attractive poster poem.

11. See Bohn, *Aesthetics of Visual Poetry*, 172–84.

12. Karl Baedeker, *Spain and Portugal: Handbook for Travelers*, 4th ed. (Leipzig: Baedeker, 1913), 390. Much of the following information is taken from this volume.

13. Gustavo Adolfo Bécquer, *Obras* (Barcelona: Vergara, 1962), 668.

Chapter 3: Hispano-American Poetry

1. Vicente Huidobro, "Triangulo armónico," "Fresco nipón," "La capilla aldeana," and "Nipona" in *Canciones en la noche* (Santiago de Chile: Chile, 1913). Repr. in *Obras completas* (Santiago de Chile: Zig-Zag, 1964), 1:158–61. The manuscripts are reproduced in René de Costa, "Trayectoria del caligrama en Huidobro," *Poesía* (Madrid), no. 3 (November-December 1978), 29–44.

2. For a detailed study of Tablada's visual poetry, see Bohn, *Modern Visual Poetry*, 156–91. The second Latin American to experiment with visual poetry was technically Marius de Zayas, who introduced Tablada to the genre in New York in 1915. However, de Zayas is associated with the history of visual poetry in the United States rather than Latin America. See Willard Bohn, *Apollinaire and the International Avant-Garde* (Albany: State University of New York Press, 1997), 48–56 and 266–71.

3. Reprinted, like the two following poems, in Luis Quintanilla, *Obra poética* (Mexico City: Domés, 1986), n.p. The device occurs twice, at the beginning and the end of the poem.

4. Guillaume Apollinaire, *Oeuvres poétiques*, ed. Marcel Adéma and Michel Décaudin (Paris: Gallimard/Pléiade, 1956), 203.

5. Salvador Novo, *Poesía, 1915–1955* (Mexico City: Impresiones Modernas, 1955), n.p.

6. Salvador Novo, "Jarrón," *Prisma* (Barcelona) no. 3 (July 1922): 172. Described as a "poema ideográfico," the poem was originally unpunctuated. The first line was in lowercase letters, the second "Bello" was capitalized, and the last line was in italics.

7. Agustín Loera y Chavez, "La poesía contemporánea mexicana," *Nosotros* 55, no. 213 (February 1927): 184. The article is dated "París, 1926."

8. See Bohn, *Modern Visual Poetry*, 73–78.

9. Apollinaire, *Oeuvres poétiques*, 203.

10. The following events are narrated in José María González de Mendoza, *Ensayos selectos* (Mexico City: Fondo de Cultura Económica, 1970), 275–77 and 279–80. Entitled "Los poemas 'al alimón' de José D. Frías," the first selection originally appeared in *Revista de Revistas* 27, no. 1416 (July 11, 1937).

11. Walter Benjamin, "The Work of Art in the Age of Mechanical Reproduction," in *Illuminations*, tr. Hannah Arendt (New York: Schocken, 1969), 217–51.

12. We know, for example, that Hidalgo spent the summer of 1920 in the Spanish capital, where he was attracted to the Ultraist movement.

13. Alberto Hidalgo, *Química del espíritu* (Buenos Aires: Mercatali, 1923).

14. Apollinaire, *Oeuvres poétiques*, 203.

15. Frantz Fanon, *Peau noire, masques blancs* (Paris: Seuil, 1952), 5.

16. Thorpe Running, *Borges' Ultraist Movement and Its Poets* (Lathrup Village, MI: International Book Publishers, 1981), 131.

17. Oliverio Girondo, *Espantapájaros: al alcance de todos* (Buenos Aires: Proa, 1932). Repr. in *Obra completa*, ed. Raúl Antelo (Barcelona: Galaxia Gutenberg, 1999), plate 15. Judging from the original typescript (reproduced in plate 15), Girondo composed the text first and devised the visual image later. For some reason, the original colored version has been replaced in subsequent editions by another version that differs from it in several respects (see *Obra completa*, 77). In the latter poem, for example, the four sections are contiguous.

18. Running, *Borges' Ultraist Movement*, 129.

19. Jorge Schwartz, "Vanguardias enfrentadas: Oliverio Girondo y la poesía concreta," in *Las vanguardias literarias en Argentina, Uruguay y Paraguay*, ed. Carlos García and Dieter Reichardt (Madrid: Iberoamericana and Frankfurt: Vervuert, 2004), 357.

Chapter 4: After Apollinaire

1. Amédée Ozenfant, "Psychotypie & typométrique," *L'Elan*, no. 9 (February 1916), inside front cover. Ozenfant claimed to be quoting an article by André Billy.

2. See for example Arthur Cohen, "The Typographic Revolution: Antecedents and Legacy of Dada Graphic Design," in *Dada Spectrum: The Dialectics of Revolt*, ed. Stephen Foster and Rudolf Kuenzli (Madison: Coda, 1979), 71–89.

3. Tristan Tzara, "BILAN," *SIC*, nos. 49–50 (October 15–30, 1919): 385. Revised and reprinted as "Sels de minuit" in *De nos oiseaux* (Paris: Kra, 1929) and *Oeuvres complètes*, ed. Henri Béhar (Paris: Flammarion, 1975), 1:201.

4. Tzara, *Oeuvres complètes*, 678.

5. André Breton, *Oeuvres complètes*, ed. Marguerite Bonnet et al. (Paris: Gallimard/Pléiade, 1988), 1:341–43.

6. See Anna Balakian, "Breton in the Light of Apollinaire," in *About French Poetry from Dada to "Tel Quel": Text and Theory*, ed. Mary Ann Caws (Detroit: Wayne State University Press, 1974), 42–53.

7. See Willard Bohn, *The Rise of Surrealism: Cubism, Dada, and the Pursuit of the Marvelous* (Albany: State University of New York Press, 2002), 121–39.

8. Breton, *Oeuvres complètes*, 1:155–56.

9. Ibid., and André Breton, *Clair de terre* (Paris: Gallimard: 1966), 47–48. The poem was originally published on facing pages, which poses a similar problem.

10. Michael Riffaterre, *Text Production*, tr. Terese Lyons (New York: Columbia University Press, 1983), 50.

11. Jean Gérard Lapacherie, "Breton critique d'Apollinaire: le calligramme comme bégaiement," in *Que Vlo-Ve?, Bulletin International des Etudes sur Apollinaire*, 2nd series, no. 14 (April–June 1985): 16–20.

12. At one point, Breton considered naming the poem "Musique." See *Oeuvres complètes,* 1195.

13. Guillermo de Torre, *Literaturas europeas de vanguardia* (Madrid: Rafael Caro Raggio, 1925), 219.

14. Breton, *Oeuvres complètes,* 1:143–44.

15. Ibid., 1180.

16. Lapacherie, "Breton critique d'Apollinaire," 18.

17. Breton, *Oeuvres complètes,* 1:41.

18. Although this resemblance is primarily stylistic, a sonnet beginning "Surgi de la croupe et du bond" ("Risen from the crupper and the bound") contains references to "une verrerie éphémère" and "le pur vase d'aucun breuvage" ("ephemeral glassware" and "the pure vase of no drink").

19. Stéphane Mallarmé, letter to Henri Cazalis written in October or November 1864, in *Correspondance,* ed. Henri Mondor and Jean-Pierre Richard (Paris: Gallimard/Pléiade, 1959), 1:137.

20. Louis Aragon, "L'Homme coupé en deux," *Les Lettres Françaises,* no. 1233 (May 9–15, 1968): 9. Alain Chevrier analyzes another visual poem from *Clair de Terre* in "Sur un poème typographique d'André Breton," *Mélusine: Cahiers du Centre de Recherche sur le Surréalisme,* no. 26 (2006): 229–45.

21. See Giovanni Lista, "Les Caractères du 'Futurisme Français' à travers l'oeuvre de Pierre Albert-Birot," in *Présence de Marinetti,* ed. Jean-Claude Marcadé (Lausanne: L'Age d'Homme, 1982), 156–75; Arlette Albert-Birot, "Pierre Albert-Birot, 'Sic' et le futurisme," *Europe,* Vol. 53, no. 551 (March 1975): 98–104; and Germana Cerenza Orlandi, "Pierre Albert-Birot, un surrealista fuori del 'Castello,'" *Quaderni del Novecento Francese,* no. 2 (1974): 75–95.

22. Guillaume Apollinaire, "Poèmepréface prophétie," *Oeuvres poétiques,* ed. Marcel Adéma and Michel Décaudin (Paris: Gallimard/Pléiade, 1965), 684. See also "Un poème," p. 360.

23. Jean Follain, *Pierre Albert-Birot* (Paris: Seghers, 1967), 22.

24. David W. Seaman, *Concrete Poetry in France* (Ann Arbor: UMI Research Press, 1981), 184.

25. Pierre Albert-Birot, *Poésie 1916–1924* (Paris: Gallimard, 1967), 337.

26. Debra Kelly, "From Painter to Poet: The Visual Poetry of Pierre Albert-Birot in *La Lune ou le livre des poèmes,*" *Forum for Modern Language Studies* 32, no. 1 (January 1996): 40.

27. Seaman, *Concrete Poetry in France,* 184.

28. Ibid., 186.

29. Guillaume Apollinaire, *Oeuvres en prose complètes,* ed. Pierre Caizergues and Michel Décaudin (Paris: Gallimard/Pléiade, 1991), 2:18.

30. Guillaume Apollinaire, "Merveille de la guerre," *Oeuvres poétiques,* ed. Adéma and Décaudin, 271.

Chapter 5: Aeropoetry

1. *Manifesto della Aeropittura,* September 22, 1929. Signed by Marinetti and eight Futurist painters.

2. See for example Enrico Crispolti, *Aeropittura futurista aeropittori* (Modena: Fonte d'Abisso, 1985); Bruno Mantura and Patrizia Rosazza Ferraris, *Futurism in Flight: "Aero-*

pittura" Paintings and Sculptures of Man's Conquest of Space (1913–1945) (Rome: De Luca, 1990); and Massimo Duranti, *Aeropittura e aeroscultura futuriste* (San Sisto: Effe, 2002).

3. F. T. Marinetti, *Manifesto dell'aeropoesia, La Gazzetta del Popolo,* October 22, 1931. A French version was published in *Stile Futurista* 1, no. 3 (September 1934).

4. Claudia Salaris, *Storia del futurismo: libri, giornali, manifesti,* rev. ed. (Rome: Editori Riuniti, 1992), 226.

5. Ignazio Scurto, "VOLO SU TRAÙ," *Futurismo* 1, no. 16 (1932).

6. F. T. Marinetti, preface to *Tavole parolibere,* by Pino Masnata (Rome: "Poesia," 1932. Quoted in Pino Masnata, *Poesia visiva: storia e teoria* (Rome: Bulzoni, 1984), 182. Several of the compositions are reprinted on pp. 329–40.

7. Pino Masnata, "AEROPLANI," *Futurismo,* April 16, 1933. Later included in *Canti fascisti della metropoli verde* (Milan: Morreale, 1935). Repr. in Masnata, *Poesia visiva,* 363

8. Masnata, *Poesia visiva,* 185.

9. See Claudio G. Segre, *Italo Balbo: A Fascist Life* (Berkeley: University of California Press, 1990).

10. F. T. Marinetti, *Manifesto tecnico della letteratura futurista,* May 11, 1912.

11. Amedeo Astori, ed., *Mostra antologica di Tullio Crali* (Trieste: Azienda Autonoma di Soggiorno e Turismo, 1976), 96.

12. Tullio Crali, preface to *Alla XXII Biennale internazionale d'arte trionfa la mostra personale di Crali* (Venice, 1940).

13. Tullio Crali, "Altalenando sulle isole dalmate," ibid. Repr. in *Crali: aeropittorefuturista* (Milan: All'Insegna del Pesce d'Oro, 1988), 72.

Chapter 6: Concrete Poetry

1. For a study of Concrete poetry in general, see Bohn, *Modern Visual Poetry,* 232–55.

2. See ibid., p. 233.

3. Augusto de Campos, Décio Pignatari, and Haroldo de Campos, "plano-pilôto para poesia concreta," *Noigandres,* no. 4 (1958). Repr. in *Concrete Poetry: A World View,* ed. Mary Ellen Solt (Bloomington: Indiana University Press, 1970), 70–71. The translation is my own.

4. See Claus Clüver, "*Klangfarbenmelodie* in Polychromatic Poems: A. von Webern and A. de Campos," *Comparative Literature Studies* 18, no. 3 (September 1981): 386–98.

5. Three of the poems in this series are reproduced on the poet's Web site at www2 .uol.com.br/augustodecampos/poemas.htm.

6. De Campos, Pignatari, and de Campos, "plano-pilôto para poesia concreta," in Solt, *Concrete Poetry,* 70.

7. Augusto de Campos, *Poesia 1949–1979* (São Paulo: Duas Cidades, 1979), n.p. The other poems examined in this chapter are also taken from this volume.

8. Augusto de Campos, "Points-Periphery-Concrete Poetry," *Jornal do Brasil,* November 11, 1956. Tr. by Jon M. Tolman and repr. in *The Avant-Garde Tradition in Literature,* ed. Richard Kostelanetz (Buffalo: Prometheus, 1982), 263.

9. One of four types of Concrete poetry identified by the "plano-piloto." See Bohn, *Modern Visual Poetry,* 237.

10. Solt, *Concrete Poetry,* 254.

11. Clüver, "*Klangfarbenmeolodie,*" 395–96. He describes the recording in detail.

12. De Campos, "Points-Periphery-Concrete Poetry," 260.

13. Quoted in Michael Webster, *Reading Visual Poetry after Futurism: Marinetti, Apollinaire, Schwitters, Cummings* (New York: Lang, 1995), 147.

14. De Campos, Pignatari, and de Campos, "plano-pilôto para poesia concreta," in Solt, *Concrete Poetry*, 71.

15. Quoted in Emmett Williams, *An Anthology of Concrete Poetry* (New York: Something Else Press, 1967), n.p.

16. Solt, *Concrete Poetry: A World View*, p. 7.

17. Quoted in Williams, *Concrete Poetry.*

18. Solt, *Concrete Poetry*, 62.

19. De Campos, "Points-Periphery-Concrete Poetry," 259.

20. K. David Jackson, "Haroldo de Campos and the Poetics of Invention," in *Haroldo de Campos: A Dialogue with the Brazilian Concrete Poet*, ed. K. David Jackson (Oxford: Oxford University Centre for Brazilian Studies, 2005), 18.

21. K. Alfons Knauth, "Palabrás: The Haroldic Emblem," in *Experimental—Visual—Concrete: Avant-Garde Poetry Since the 1960s*, ed. K. David Jackson, Eric Vos, and Johanna Drucker (Amsterdam: Rodopi, 1996), 157.

22. Solt, *Concrete Poetry*, 13.

23. De Campos, Pignatari, and de Campos, "plano-pilôto," in Solt, *Concrete Poetry*, 71.

24. Haroldo de Campos, *Xadrez de estrelas: percurso textual 1949–1974* (São Paulo: Perspectiva, 1976), n.p. The other poems examined in this chapter are also taken from this volume.

25. Philadelpho Menezes, *Poetics and Visuality: A Trajectory of Contemporary Brazilian Poetry*, tr. Harry Polkinhorn (San Diego: San Diego State University Press, 1994), 25.

26. Claus Clüver, "Reflections on Verbivocovisual Ideograms," *Poetics Today* 3, no. 3 (1982), p. 138.

27. Claus Clüver, "Concrete Poetry: Critical Perspectives from the 90s," in *Experimental—Visual—Concrete*, ed. Jackson, Vos, and Drucker, 272.

28. Quoted in Williams, *Concrete Poetry.*

29. Stuart Flexner and Doris Flexner, *Wise Words and Wives' Tales: The Origins, Meanings, and Time-Honored Wisdom of Proverbs and Folk Sayings Olde and New* (New York: Avon, 1993).

30. For two additional interpretations, see Marjorie Perloff, "Concrete Prose in the Nineties: Harold de Campos's *Galáxias* and After," in *Haroldo de Campos*, ed. Jackson, 141.

31. See the diagram at the website, http://cst-www.nrl.navy.mil/lattice/struk/Te.html.

32. Décio Pignatari, *Poesia pois é poesia, 1950–1975* (São Paulo: Duas Cidades, 1977), 84.

33. Iumna Maria Simon and Vinicius Dantas, *Poesia concreta* (São Paulo: April, 1982), n.p.

34. José Lino Grünewald, *Escreviver* (Rio de Janeiro: Nova Fronteira, 1987), 66. The other poems examined in this chapter are also taken from this volume.

Chapter 7: Digital Poetry

1. Johanna Drucker, "Experimental, Visual, and Concrete Poetry: A Note on Historical Context and Basic Concepts," in *Experimental—Visual—Concrete*, ed. Jackson, Vos, and Drucker, 58.

2. Giselle Beiguelman, "Nomadic Poems," in *Media Poetry: An International Anthology*, ed. Eduardo Kac (Bristol: Intellect Books, 2007), 99.

3. Eduardo Kac, "From ASCII to Cyberspace: A Trajectory in Digital Poetry," in Kac, *Media Poetry*, 45. Cited in the text hereafter as MP.

4. Kac is quick to distinguish between these two modes. Unless one has experienced a video composition in its original state, he declares, it is difficult to appreciate the difference that computerization introduces. "Which is to say," he continues, "that most works explore/produce different modalities of spatiotemporal experiences (including, runtime, loop, interactive, navigational, multiuser, etc.). In some cases I even use *light* semantically" (conversation with the author May 21, 2009). Although most of the works discussed here were originally video installations, computerized versions may be viewed at www.ekac.org/multimedia.html. Cited in the text henceforth as "EKAC."

5. Eduardo Kac, conversation with the author May 5, 2009.

6. J. E. Cirlot, *A Dictionary of Symbols*, tr. Jack Sage, 2nd ed. (London: Routledge Kegan Paul, 1971), 2.

Chapter 8: Eyesight and Insight

1. Johanna Drucker, *The Visible Word: Experimental Typography and Modern Art, 1909–1923* (Chicago: University of Chicago Press, 1994), 10.

2. Rudolf Arnheim, *Visual Thinking* (Berkeley: University of California Press, 1969), 233–34.

3. Betty Edwards, *Drawing on the Right Side of the Brain*, rev. ed. (New York: Putnam, 1989), 30.

4. J. E. Bogen, "Some Educational Aspects of Hemisphere Specialization," *UCLA Educator*, No. 17 (1975), 24–32.

5. For example, a camera's adjustable aperture is called an "iris."

6. Concerning the "duck-rabbit" conundrum, see W. J. T. Mitchell, *Picture Theory* (Chicago: University of Chicago Press, 1994), 45–57. For the second example, see Edwards, *Drawing on the Right Side of the Brain*, 46.

7. Arnheim, *Visual Thinking*, 14.

8. Edwards, *Drawing on the Right Side of the Brain*, 30.

9. Arnheim, *Art and Visual Perception*, 46.

Bibliography

Albert-Birot, Arlette. "Pierre Albert-Birot, 'Sic' et le futurisme." *Europe*, 53, no. 551 (March 1975): 98–104.

Albert-Birot, Pierre. *Poésie 1916–1924.* Paris: Gallimard, 1967.

Alvarez Serrano, Ramón. "La preconsulta del Dr. Wollman." *Grecia,* February 20, 1920.

Apollinaire, Guillaume. *Oeuvres en prose complètes.* Edited by Michel Décaudin and Pierre Caizergues. 3 vols. Paris: Gallimard/Pléiade, 1977–93.

———. *Oeuvres poétiques.* Edited Marcel Adéma and Michel Décaudin. Paris: Gallimard/ Pléiade, 1965.

Aragon, Louis. "L'Homme coupé en deux." *Les Lettres Françaises,* no. 1233 (May 9–15, 1968): 3–9.

Arnheim, Rudolf. *Art and Visual Perception: A Psychology of the Creative Eye.* Rev. ed. Berkeley: University of California Press, 1974.

———. *Visual Thinking.* Berkeley: University of California Press, 1969.

Astori, Amedeo, ed. *Mostra antologica di Tullio Crali.* Trieste: Azienda Autonoma di Soggiorno e Turismo, 1976.

Baedeker, Karl. *Spain and Portugal: Handbook for Travelers.* 4th ed. Leipzig: Baedeker, 1913.

Balakian, Anna. "Breton in the Light of Apollinaire." In *About French Poetry from Dada to "Tel Quel": Text and Theory,* edited by Mary Ann Caws, 42–53. Detroit: Wayne State University Press, 1974.

Bautista, Juan. "Revelación." *Grecia,* December 31, 1919.

Bécquer, Gustavo Adolfo. *Obras.* Barcelona: Vergara, 1962.

Beiguelman, Giselle. "Nomadic Poems." In *Media Poetry: An International Anthology,* edited by Eduardo Kac, 97–103. Bristol: Intellect Books, 2007.

Benjamin, Walter. *Illuminations.* Translated by Hannah Arendt. New York: Schocken, 1969.

Bogen, J. E. "Some Educational Aspects of Hemisphere Specialization." *UCLA Educator,* no. 17 (1975): 24–32.

Bohn, Willard. *The Aesthetics of Visual Poetry, 1914–1928.* Cambridge: Cambridge University Press, 1986; Chicago: University of Chicago Press, 1993.

———. *Apollinaire and the International Avant-Garde.* Albany: State University of New York Press, 1997.

———. *Modern Visual Poetry.* Newark: University of Delaware Press, 2001.

———. *The Rise of Surrealism: Cubism, Dada, and the Pursuit of the Marvelous.* Albany: State University of New York Press, 2002.

Breton, André. *Clair de terre.* Paris: Gallimard, 1966.

———. *Oeuvres complètes*. Ed. Marguerite Bonnet et al. 3 vols. Paris: Gallimard/Pléiade, 1988–1999.

Buendía, Rogelio. "Rayos X." *Grecia*, February 20, 1920.

Campos, Augusto de. *Poesia 1949–1979*. São Paulo: Duas Cidades, 1979.

———. "Points-Periphery-Concrete Poetry." *Jornal do Brasil*, November 11, 1956. Reprinted in *The Avant-Garde Tradition in Literature*. Edited by Richard Kostelanetz, translated by Jon M. Tolman, 259–66. Buffalo: Prometheus, 1982.

———. Website. www2.uol.com.br/augustodecampos/poemas.htm.

Campos, Augusto de, Décio Pignatari, and Haroldo de Campos. "plano-pilôto para poesia concreta." *Noigandres*, no. 4 (1958). Reprinted in *Concrete Poetry: A World View*, edited by Mary Ellen Solt, 70–71. Bloomington: Indiana University Press, 1970).

Campos, Haroldo de. *Xadrez de estrelas: percurso textual 1949–1974*. São Paulo: Perspectiva, 1976.

Cangiullo, Francesco. "Fumatori II." *Lacerba* 2, no. 1 (January 1914): 10–11.

Cansinos-Asséns, Rafael. *La nueva literatura*. 4 vols. Madrid: Paéz, 1927.

Chevrier, Alain. "Sur un poème typographique d'André Breton." *Mélusine: Cahiers du Centre de Recherche sur le Surréalisme*, no. 26 (2006): 229–45.

Cirlot, J. E. *A Dictionary of Symbols*. Translated by Jack Sage. 2nd ed. London: Routledge Kegan Paul, 1971.

Clüver, Claus. "Concrete Poetry: Critical Perspectives from the 90s." *Experimental—Visual—Concrete: Avant-Garde Poetry Since the 1960s*. Edited by K. David Jackson, Eric Vos, and Johanna Drucker, 265–85. Amsterdam: Rodopi, 1996.

———. "*Klangfarbenmelodie* in Polychromatic Poems: A. von Webern and A. de Campos." *Comparative Literature Studies* 28, no. 3 (September 1981): 386–98.

———. "Reflections on Verbivocovisual Ideograms." *Poetics Today* 3, no. 3 (1982): 137–48.

Cohen, Arthur. "The Typographic Revolution: Antecedents and Legacy of Dada Graphic Design." in *Dada Spectrum: The Dialectics of Revolt*, edited by Stephen Foster and Rudolf Kuenzli, 71–89. Madison: Coda, 1979.

Costa, René de. "Trayectoria del caligrama en Huidobro." *Poesía* (Madrid), no. 3 (November–December 1978): 27–44.

Crali, Tullio. *Crali: aeropittorefuturista*. Milan: All'Insegna del Pesce d'Oro, 1988.

———. *Alla XXII Biennale internazionale d'arte trionfa la mostra personale di Crali: Nuova grande vittoria dell'aeropittura italiana primato plastico sopravanzante le pitture estere e primato nella glorificazione aeropittorica della veloce bombardante guerra aerea*. Venice 1940.

Crispolti, Enrico. *Aeropittura futurista aeropittori*. Modena: Fonte d'Abisso, 1985.

Curtius, Ernst Robert. *European Literature and the Latin Middle Ages*. Translated by Willard Trask. New York: Harper and Row, 1953.

Dada Almanach. Edited by Richard Huelsenbeck. Berlin: Reiss, 1920.

Drucker, Johanna. "Experimental, Visual, and Concrete Poetry: A Note on Historical Context and Basic Concepts." In *Experimental—Visual—Concrete: Avant-Garde Poetry since the 1960s*, edited by K. David Jackson, Eric Vos, and Johanna Drucker, 39–61. Amsterdam: Rodopi, 1996.

———. *The Visible Word: Experimental Typography and Modern Art, 1909–1923*. Chicago: University of Chicago Press, 1994.

Duranti, Massimo. *Aeropittura e aeroscultura futuriste*. San Sisto: Effe, 2002.

Edwards, Betty. *Drawing on the Right Side of the Brain*. Rev. ed. New York: Putnam, 1989.

Edwards, Jacques. "Aviador Dada." *Grecia*, January 20, 1920.

Fanon, Frantz. *Peau noire, masques blancs*. Paris: Seuil, 1952.

Flexner, Stuart, and Doris Flexner. *Wise Words and Wives' Tales: The Origins, Meanings, and Time-Honored Wisdom of Proverbs and Folk Sayings Olde and New*. New York: Avon, 1993.

Follain, Jean. *Pierre Albert-Birot*. Paris: Seghers, 1967.

Girondo, Oliverio. *Espantapájaros: al alcance de todos*. Buenos Aires: Proa, 1932.

———. *Obra completa*. Edited by Raúl Antelo. Barcelona: Galaxia Gutenberg, 1999.

Gonzalez de Mendoza, José María. *Ensayos selectos*. Mexico City: Fondo de Cultura Económica, 1970.

———. "Los poemas 'al alimón' de José D. Frías." *Revista de Rivistas* 28, no. 1416 (July 11, 1937).

Grünewald, José Lino. *Escreviver*. Rio de Janeiro: Nova Fronteira, 1987.

Hidalgo, Alberto. *Química del espíritu*. Buenos Aires: Mercatali, 1923.

Huidobro, Vicente. *Canciones en la noche*. Santiago de Chile: Chile, 1913.

———. *Obras completas*. 2 vols. Santiago de Chile: Zig-Zag, 1964.

Jackson, K. David, ed. *Haroldo de Campos: A Dialogue with the Brazilian Concrete Poet* (Oxford: Oxford University Centre for Brazilian Studies, 2005).

———. "Haroldo de Campos and the Poetics of Invention." In *Haroldo de Campos: A Dialogue with the Brazilian Concrete Poet*, edited by K. David Jackson, 17–25. Oxford: Oxford University Centre for Brazilian Studies, 2005.

Kac, Eduardo. "From ASCII to Cyberspace: A Trajectory in Digital Poetry." In *Media Poetry: An International Anthology*, edited by Eduardo Kac, 45–65. (Bristol and Chicago: Intellect Books, 2007.

Kelly, Debra. "From Painter to Poet: The Visual Poetry of Pierre Albert-Birot in *La Lune ou le livre des poèmes*." *Forum for Modern Language Studies*, 32, no. 1 (January 1996): 37–54.

Knauth, K. Alfons. "Palabrás: The Haroldic Emblem." In *Experimental—Visual—Concrete: Avant-Garde Poetry Since the 1960s*, edited by K. David Jackson, Eric Vos, and Johanna Drucker, 157–72. Amsterdam: Rodopi, 1996.

Lapacherie, Jean Gérard. "Breton critique d'Apollinaire: le calligramme comme bégaiement." *Que Vlo-Ve?: Bulletin International des Etudes sur Apollinaire*, 2nd series, no. 14 (April–June 1985): 16–20.

Lista, Giovanni. "Les Caractères du 'Futurisme Français' à travers l'oeuvre de Pierre Albert-Birot." In *Présence de Marinetti*, edited by Jean-Claude Marcadé, 156–75. Lausanne: L'Age d'Homme, 1982.

Loera y Chavez, Agustín. "La poesía contemporánea mexicana." *Nosotros* 55, no. 213 (February 10, 1927): 184.

Mallarmé, Stéphane. *Correspondance*. Edited by Henri Mondor and Lloyd James Austin. 12 vols. Paris: Gallimard/Pléiade, 1959–85.

Mantura, Bruno, and Patrizia Rosazza Ferraris. *Futurism in Flight: "Aeropittura" Paintings and Sculptures of Man's Conquest of Space (1913–1945)*. Rome: De Luca, 1990.

Marinetti, F. T. "Manifeste de l'aeropoésie." *Stile Futurista* 1, no. 3 (September 1934).

———. "Manifesto dell'aeropoesia." *La Gazzetta del Popolo*, October 22, 1931.

———. *Manifesto tecnico della letteratura futurista*, May 11, 1912.

———. Preface to *Tavole parolibere*, by Pino Masnata. Rome: "Poesia," 1932.

Marinetti, F. T., and Pino Masnata. *Manifesto futurista della radio*. 1933.

Marinetti, F. T., et al. *Manifesto della Aeropittura.* September 22, 1929.

Masnata, Pino. "AEROPLANI." *Futurismo,* April 16, 1933.

———. *Canti fascisti della metropoli verde.* Milan: Morreale, 1935.

———. *Poesia visiva: storia e teoria.* Rome: Bulzoni, 1984.

———. *Tavole parolibere.* Rome: "Poesia," 1932.

Masnata, Pino, and F. T. Marinetti. *Manifesto futurista della radio.* 1933.

Menezes, Philadelpho. *Poetics and Visuality: A Trajectory of Contemporary Brazilian Poetry.* Tranlsated by Harry Polkinhorn. San Diego: San Diego State University Press, 1994.

Mitchell, W. J. T. *Picture Theory.* Chicago: University of Chicago Press, 1994.

———. *What Do Pictures Want?: The Lives and Loves of Images.* Chicago: University of Chicago Press, 2005.

Morand, Paul. "Antología: en la Puerta del Sol." Translated by Rafael Cansinos-Asséns. *Grecia,* June 10, 1919.

Nimero, Andrés. "Poema alfa de la gran circunvalación." *Grecia,* October 12, 1919.

Novo, Salvador. "Jarrón." *Prisma* (Barcelona), vol. 2, no. 3 (July 1922): 172.

———. *Poesía, 1915–1955.* Mexico City: Impresiones Modernas, 1955.

Orlandi, Germana Cerenza. "Pierre Albert-Birot, un surrealista fuori del 'Castello.'" *Quaderni del Novecento Francese,* no. 2 (1974): 75–95.

Ozenfant, Amédée. "Psychotypie & typométrique." *L'Elan,* no. 9 (February 1916): inside front cover.

Perloff, Marjorie. "Concrete Prose in the Nineties: Haroldo de Campos's *Galáxias* and After." in *Haroldo de Campos: A Dialogue with the Brazilian Concrete Poet,* edited by K. David Jackson, 139–61. Oxford: Oxford University Centre for Brazilian Studies, 2005.

———. *Radical Artifice: Writing Poetry in the Age of Media.* Chicago: University of Chicago Press, 1991.

Pignatari, Décio. *Poesia pois é poesia, 1950–1975.* São Paulo: Duas Cidades, 1977.

The Poem Generator. www.vita.uwnet.nl/poem/poem.html.

Puche, Eliodoro. "Silencio." *Ultra,* May 21, 1921.

Quintanilla, Luis. *Obra poética.* Mexico City: Domés, 1986.

Raida, Pedro. "EL FUTURO NIDO." *Grecia,* November 20, 1919.

———. "En el seno de los modernos atletas del canto." *Grecia,* January 20, 1920.

Riffaterre, Michael. *Text Production.* Translated by Terese Lyons. New York: Columbia University Press, 1983.

Rigolot, François. "Le Poétique et l'analogique." *Poétique,* no. 35 (September 1978): 257–68.

Running, Thorpe. *Borges' Ultraist Movement and Its Poets.* Lathrup Village, MI: International Book Publishers, 1981.

The Sackner Archive of Concrete and Visual Poetry. http://www.rediscov.com/sackner-archives/.

Salaris, Claudia. *Storia del futurismo: libri, giornali, manifesti.* Rev. ed. Rome: Editori Riuniti, 1992.

Schwartz, Jorge. "Vanguardias enfrentadas: Oliverio Girondo y la poesía concreta." In *Las vanguardias literarias en Argentina, Uruguay y Paraguay.* Ed. Carlos García and Dieter Reichardt, Madrid: Iberoamericana and Frankfurt: Vervuert, 2004.

Scurto, Ignazio. "VOLO SU TRAÙ." *Futurismo,* 1, no. 16 (1932).

Seaman, David W. *Concrete Poetry in France*. Ann Arbor: UMI Research Press, 1981.

Segre, Claudio G. *Italo Balbo: A Fascist Life*. Berkeley: University of California Press, 1990.

Silva, Goy de. "Silencio." *Cervantes*, February 1919.

Simon, Iumna Maria, and Vinicius Dantas. *Poesia concreta*. São Paulo: April, 1982.

Tablada, Jose Juan. *Li-Po y otros poemas*. Caracas: Bolívar, 1920.

Torre, Guillermo de. *Guillaume Apollinaire: estudio preliminar y páginas escogidas*. Buenos Aires: Poseidon, 1946.

———. *Hélices, poemas (1918–1922)*. Madrid: Mundo Latino, 1923.

———. *Literaturas europeas de vanguardia*. Madrid: Rafael Caro Raggio, 1925.

Tzara, Tristan. "BILAN," *SIC*, nos. 49–50 (October 15–30, 1919): 385.

———. *De nos oiseaux*. Paris: Kra, 1929.

———. *Oeuvres complètes*. Edited by Henri Béhar. 6 vols. Paris: Flammarion, 1975.

Valle, Adriano del. "Signo celeste." *Grecia*, December 20, 1919.

Vando-Villar, Isaac del. "En el infierno de una noche." *Grecia*, October 30, 1919.

Videla, Gloria. *El Ultraísmo*. 2nd ed. Madrid: Gredos, 1971.

Vighi, Francisco. "CELESTIALES FUEGOS ARTIFICIALES." *Reflector*, December 1920.

Webster, Michael. *Reading Visual Poetry after Futurism: Marinetti, Apollinaire, Schwitters, Cummings*. New York: Lang, 1995.

Williams, Emmett. *An Anthology of Concrete Poetry*. New York: Something Else Press, 1967.

Index

www.ingramcontent.com/pod-product-compliance
Lightning Source LLC
Chambersburg PA
CBHW071520100726
47908CB00004B/1240

9781611476156